The Historic Towns of Britain

The Historic Towns of Britain

Lewis Braithwaite

Adam & Charles Black · London

British Library Cataloguing in Publication Data

Braithwaite, Lewis
The historic towns of Britain.
1. Great Britain – Gazetteers
2. Cities and towns – Great Britain
I. Title
914.1′003   DA640

ISBN 0-7136-2118-4

Published by A & C Black (Publishers) Limited,
35 Bedford Row, London WC1R 4JH

ISBN 0 7136 2118 4

First published 1981
© 1981 Lewis Braithwaite

Filmset and printed in Great Britain by
BAS Printers Limited, Over Wallop, Hampshire

Contents

Introduction

Why a book on historic towns at all?

One of the most striking features of the last two decades has been the growth of interest in conservation, and in particular the environment and townscape of our historic towns. This is shown by the founding of the Civic Trust in 1956, the formation (by 1980) of 1250 amenity societies registered with it, by local guidebooks beginning to give 'Walks round the town' or 'Town trails' to supplement their traditional list of vicars and borough charters; and by the increased space given to this in each successive volume of Sir Nikolaus Pevsner's 'Buildings of England' series.

Yet despite this interest there is no general one volume guide to British historic towns, which is what this book attempts to provide. The main national topographical guides, such as the 'Blue Guides', do now occasionally mention a town as having many historic buildings and streets, but they concentrate on the major individual tourist attractions: major historic monuments such as the cathedral, abbey church, or castle; major historic houses open to the public, including some of the great mansions of the aristocracy, and interesting collections such as art galleries and museums. This book largely ignores these, not because they are unimportant but because they are already well dealt with. This book is envisaged as one you might have at home or in the car alongside the 'Blue Guide', but not instead of it.

The basic reason for this book is my desire to share with others the enjoyment and pleasure I feel when wandering round and exploring historic towns. I find historic towns not only interesting historically, but attractive as an urban environment. Like the canals, my other main interest, they are a major man-made legacy from the past—a world of intimacy, textures, materials, attractive details, human scale, to be enjoyed all the more when confronted by a modern built environment that is often hostile, faceless and inhuman in scale.

The bulk of the book is a Gazetteer guide, which will try to indicate which towns to explore, and which parts and streets to concentrate on. The write-ups are less detailed than the later Pevsner Perambulations in the 'Buildings of England' series, but in any case looking at townscape and streets is not necessarily the same as looking at a town's most interesting buildings—even if one has a car glove compartment and a purse to accommodate all 46 Pevsner volumes.

The first chapter 'What is a Historic Town?' defines the towns chosen for the Gazetteer. It does not include at one end of the population scale urban villages, which may historically have been towns but are really now villages—places like Chipping Campden, Broadway or Thaxted. These are already unpleasantly chockablock with tourist coaches in the summer months, largely because they are thought of as 'pretty villages' rather than as towns. And at the other extreme what I call historic cities are excluded— because big cities, whatever their origin, are a different animal anyway, because certain famous historic cities like York and Norwich are so extensive they need to be tackled in several perambulations on several days and because others like Oxford, Cambridge and Bath are well covered already. So the largest towns covered are Exeter (90,900 without Topsham), Colchester (76,531) and Worcester (73,452)—with most of the towns less than 20,000 (1971 population figures).

If readers are sceptical of my assumption that historic towns are attractive, or of my selection, I am not going to try and convince them with flowery verbal descriptions in this book. When I give an evening class on Historic Towns, I try to get the class out on a field visit to a historic town as soon as possible, and pray for good weather. I point out things to the group as we walk around, I choose my favourite streets and in my opinion the best direction to approach them and I hope people will have as much pleasure from exploring say Lichfield, as I do. In this book, not being able to take the reader personally round a historic town, all I can do is to select towns in the Gazetteer for him to visit and try to show him what to look for. If he does not like what he sees, there is nothing more I can do.

It might be thought that, as the pleasures of exploring a historic town come from using one's eyes, these can be described in a book with much visual material such as drawings and photographs. But, whereas the narrow British canals fit ideally into the camera viewfinder, one of the major attractions of historic towns—the feeling of enclosure given by building lines usually much farther apart than the 40-foot width of the canal—is almost impossible to photograph; and photographs of streets tend to look either 'crowded' if they include lots of people, or 'dead' if they don't. No picture in a book can convey the dynamic experience of walking round a historic town—the fact that as one moves, the vistas and the interrelation of buildings and the spaces between them are always changing.

So the Gazetteer contains 134 illustrations of historic towns that are not photographs of buildings but maps, the First Edition Ordnance Survey, six inches to a mile (1:10,560) published between 1848 and 1891. The best a book can do to convey the actual experience of wandering around is for readers to imagine themselves as ants moving round these maps. I hope you will find these historic maps as interesting and exciting as I do, worth poring over at home even if you are not about to visit the towns. Numbers have been inserted to enable people to use these maps for the perambulations.

It is hoped that this book will interest a wide range of people: anyone aware of their physical environment in towns and the architects and planners and councillors involved in preserving and enhancing (or destroying) it; historians wanting to extend their appreciation of buildings and street patterns which are just as much part of a town's history as are documents (the approach pioneered by W G Hoskins); those who live or work in the towns listed in the Gazetteer, to give them an outsider's view which they might then question and improve upon for themselves; and tourists, whether British or foreign, to encourage them to stop in certain towns and spend an hour or two, a morning, or a full day, or when visiting a cathedral city to extend their tour beyond the cathedral and precinct to the town.

The book covers Scotland and Wales as well as England (unlike Pevsner, though the first volumes of comparable 'Buildings of Scotland' and 'Buildings of Wales' have now been published — *Lothian* in 1978 and *Powys* in 1979). Both countries have many delightful historic towns which tend to be overlooked in the tourist emphasis on their mountains and scenery. For better or worse, I have visited all the towns described myself; so this book reflects the judgements and likes (particularly giant pilasters!) of *one* observer. This should give the book more unity than a team could have achieved, and you will doubtless come to discount any idiosyncrasies.

I naturally hope people enjoy their explorations; but I will not worry that people do not always share my enthusiasms, if they have in the process noticed new things, found new alleys, or raised their eyes above fascia level.

Happy viewing!

1 What is a Historic Town?

The two essential ingredients

I do feel there is a special type of town we can call a 'historic town', as opposed to new towns, industrial towns, large ports, Lancashire cotton towns, Yorkshire wool towns, railway centres, South Wales mining areas, suburbs and suburban-type towns—categories proposed in Moser and Scott's classic 1961 study of British Towns.

However much urban geographers and local historians may insist that as *all* towns develop and change over the years, *all* towns are 'historic', even Harlow New Town founded in 1947, a more selective definition is needed. So I distinguish between towns with historic elements or even the occasional historic monument or site, and a historic town, which requires the survival of two key elements from historic times: a large number of historic buildings in its main town centre streets, and its historic street pattern and frontages.

These historic buildings are usually small-scale houses rather than the better known parish churches, cathedrals, castles, noblemen's great houses or civic buildings such as town halls. They can be taken as the Historic Buildings listed as Grades I, II*, II on the Department of the Environment Statutory List, and until recently Grade III on its Provisional List. These categories include any timberframe or medieval building of which a substantial part remains, and almost all Georgian and Regency buildings surviving substantially unaltered. Almost all surviving buildings built before about 1840 are now listed, and one could take this date as the end of 'historic' times. Certainly the Victorian era with its rapid expansion of many towns (aided by public transport), its use of standardised building materials and its vast working-class housing areas, marks the end of the most attractive features of many towns.

Listed pre-1840 historic buildings are to be found in historic towns in some quantity. In central Ludlow there are only two buildings not listed at all. Often forming complete streets, they are always attractive, not only for their individual merits but for the way they are grouped together. Increasingly the DoE takes group value into account, often making a building that would perhaps only be Grade III in isolation Grade II because it is on a corner and a key element in the townscape of several streets, or because it is next to a Grade I or II*. The DoE does list some Victorian buildings and indeed some up to 1939, but they are very selective here, concentrating on key public buildings, such as town halls and corn exchanges, or the works of important architects: these tend to be churches and villas in the wealthier Victorian suburbs outside the historic core. This historic core is the extent of the town in say 1840, and is the basis of the walks described in the Gazetteer. When we speak of a historic town, we really mean a historic town centre which survives in some completeness, though one of the attractive features of historic towns is that they often have far less Victorian or even twentieth century suburban housing growth than most other towns, so the historic town centre is sometimes almost the complete town.

The second key element in a historic town is the survival of the street pattern or ground-plan from 'historic times'—which is why the Gazetteer includes the Victorian maps. The street pattern of a historic town can be studied to provide evidence of the origins, development or decay of the town often as valuable as the better-known documentary sources; but it is important also because it creates for us now, in the 1980s, an attractive urban environment. Unlike most modern streets, most historic street patterns give a variety of spaces between the building frontages—sometimes picturesque higgledy-piggledy lanes and alleys, sometimes opening out into little squares or fine broad streets. The actual frontages are usually pleasingly irregular in having a mixture of historic building types, in the buildings not being all in the same plane or lined up—often in broad cigar shaped streets having a gentle curve. Usually these streets have a unity and consistent human scale from the frontage lengths being surprisingly uniform—often dating from when the burgage plots were consciously laid out in medieval times (see Chapter 2).

Generally speaking if a town preserves many historic houses along its streets, it automatically preserves its street frontage also. But occasionally a street can have a strong historic character and attractive townscape with many buildings of different ages that are not necessarily listed. The buildings may be Victorian, 1930s or 1960s, but nonetheless if the streetline has been kept, without the setbacks of borough surveyors' 'improvement' lines, and if each burgage plot has been developed differently and not merged, the street can have an attractively varied townscape and strong historic character even though few buildings are technically listed. Bridge Street in Evesham is a good example. Until recently the City of London had a strong medieval character from its alleys and courts, which survived from its medieval plan, although almost all of the buildings were late 19th and 20th century.

The Council for British Archaeology list of historic towns

Fortunately I am not alone in believing that there are 'historic towns'; in 1965 the Council for British Archaeology (CBA) produced a list still recognised as the best national definition. It includes two places now in London (Richmond listed under Surrey and Chiswick under Middlesex) and 322 others (230 in England, 57 in Scotland, 35 in Wales) classified according to the following criteria:

1 Town-plan well preserved (e.g. street-plan, market place)
   a: Ancient   b: Georgian   c: Victorian
2 Bridge crossing and approaches
   a: Ancient   b: Georgian
3 Waterfront
4 Town-wall, ditch or gates well preserved
5 Castle site or precinct well preserved
6 Major ecclesiastical site or precinct well preserved
   (e.g. cathedral, abbey, etc)
7 Towns characterised by a number of buildings worthy of preservation
   a: Medieval to 17th century   b: Georgian and Regency
   c: Victorian

Thus the annotation 1a, 7ab for Chipping Norton, Oxfordshire, indicates that it has an ancient town plan with medieval and Georgian buildings.

Numbers 1 and 7 are the two criteria I regard as essential; of the CBA 322, 296 (92%) have entries under both 1 and 7. Historic buildings tend to line historic streets. Sometimes the street pattern and buildings date from the same time, but usually, though the plan is medieval, the buildings left in the streets now are Georgian (often a Georgian front over an earlier timberframe) or even Victorian. This emphasis on the town plan was the most important feature of the CBA list. Preservation before then had normally been piecemeal preservation of individual historic buildings, and the demands of traffic had caused new roads to be blitzed against the grain of the street-pattern.

Let us now look at the other criteria. Major cathedrals, abbeys and castles are the main tourist attractions of many historic towns, yet less than half of the CBA 322 have an entry under 5 or 6. The bridge crossing and approaches are an important element in many historic towns, and in some cases (though not as many as once thought) it was the strategic reason for the town being sited where it is, and for its growth. Waterfront is the key element in historic ports and seaside resorts; of the twenty-six places which do not combine 7 with 1, eleven have 7 with 3 instead: the waterfront is the historic street pattern. Finally, the town wall, a most important symbol of a town's importance in medieval times, and surprisingly little known about today. Most people know about the town walls of York, Chester and Conway, but how many people know of and have explored the fine and extensive stretches in Canterbury, Southampton, Great Yarmouth, Norwich, Tenby, Caernarvon, Berwick-on-Tweed and Newcastle-upon-Tyne?

The CBA short list

From its general list, the CBA then selected a short list of 51 towns 'so splendid and so precious that the ultimate responsibility should be a *national* concern', ie the responsibility of central rather than local government. This recognises the clash there is in almost every historic town between the interests of local people who want the same apparent growth, opportunities and 'progress' as other (non-historic) towns, and the interests of outsiders and tourists.

The short list towns should be thought of as part of a European heritage, alongside Urbino, Salzburg, Dubrovnik and Venice. They include the well-known historic cities of Bath and Edinburgh; Oxford and Cambridge; York, Norwich, Lincoln, plus, more surprisingly, the regional capitals of Newcastle-upon-Tyne and Aberdeen. At the other extreme, the famous urban villages of Chipping Campden and Burford in the Cotswolds; Thaxted and Lavenham in East Anglia; and Culross, Inveraray and Cromarty in Scotland. More typical in size, and less well-known are Pershore, Hadleigh and Barnard Castle.

Thirty-two of the short list towns are included in the Gazetteer with maps. Some are famous—the cathedral cities of Salisbury, Wells and Hereford; the abbey town of Tewkesbury; the Cinque ports of Rye and Sandwich; the castle towns of Ludlow and Warwick; Stamford and Bradford-on-Avon; Stirling, Haddington and Kelso in Scotland; Conway, Monmouth and Tenby in Wales. But others are not considered by many of their inhabitants as historic towns at all, let alone as of European importance: Totnes, Blandford Forum, Marlborough, Bridgnorth, Newark, Abingdon, Lewes; in East Anglia King's Lynn, Wymondham, Wisbech and Colchester; in Cumbria Whitehaven and Cockermouth; and in Yorkshire Richmond, Beverley and Scarborough.

This short list also upsets some judgements about which are the most important towns within certain counties; despite Shakespearian associations the CBA does not consider Stratford-upon-Avon as valuable a historic town as Warwick.

'Small is beautiful'

The 322 places on the CBA general list form the basis of the Gazetteer and are marked in the index, so their names will not be given here. Let us now look at their geographical distribution across the country, and the first indicator most people use to describe a place—population size.

The 322 occur neither in proportion to the population nor evenly across the country. There are few in industrial areas such as Glamorgan and the Scottish coalfield and none at all in the new Metropolitan Counties, whereas the new rural counties of North Yorkshire and Cumbria have 12 and 15 respectively, and Norfolk—prosperous in medieval and Georgian times, and since then remote and rural and grown relatively little (until very recent times)—has 14 places on the list, as has nearby Suffolk. Looking now at their 1971 population, 281 had less than 40,000 people.

Under 5000	130
5000– 9999	67
10,000–14,999	37
15,000–19,999	20
20,000–24,999	10
25,000–29,999	8
30,000–34,999	6
35,000–39,999	3

Why should most of the CBA places be so small? Why should there be a contradiction between a town being big and it being a historic town? It is because the factor that destroys historic town centres more than any other is growth of the town since the 'historic' times when the bulk of the historic buildings we enjoy were built. In 1967 an analysis of the 1801 and 1961 population of the 51 places on the CBA Short List showed an average growth in population of less than × 5. Twenty-two had not even doubled, four had actually got smaller, and only seventeen had increased more than × 6.

So for a town to get on to the list, two factors seem to be required:

1. Sufficient wealth and importance to have grown into a thriving town in 'historic' times (usually the medieval or Georgian period) and for numerous historic buildings to have been built.
2. Comparative stagnation or low growth since that period, to ensure that 'buildings worthy of preservation' are not subsequently destroyed, to be replaced by new shops or other town-centre uses.

It is subsequent high growth, causing their centres to be redeveloped either in Victorian times or later, that has prevented towns such as Leicester or Coventry, undoubtedly important and prosperous in 'historic times', from surviving to appear on the CBA list today: Coventry grew from 1801 to 1961 by a factor of × 20.8 and Leicester by × 16.9.

The characteristics of historic towns

We can now deduce other criteria besides the CBA's seven. Historic towns are not found in the main industrial areas and conurbations, but in rural areas. They are mostly small, comparatively unspoilt country market towns, often still fulfilling their historic economic function as centres of agriculture. Because of this, the towns cannot occur too closely together but must have a catchment area; in Dorset, where almost every town appears on the CBA list, they are 10–15 miles apart.

'Unspoilt' implies that certain destructive planning changes such as high growth and new urban roads have not taken place or have been rejected, so to some extent whether a town stays a historic town or destroys itself is a conscious choice made by local people and their local government machinery. It may depend on whether professional people live in the town, whether people are attracted to come and live in it because it is a historic town, and whether there is a lively and influential Civic Amenities Society. A historic town does not have to be peopled by wealthy widows or retired bank managers (as at Southwold) to survive, but conversely if a town is almost entirely working class, it is unlikely to have an effective civic society or be able to resist the false lure of 'growth' and 'progress', and will probably not last much longer as a historic town.

Another possible definition is whether the complete town centres are designated Conservation Areas, but the quality and purposes of these vary very considerably. It is significant if a town centre is *not* a Conservation Area (like Gloucester or Exeter) or is split up into lots of little ones like Bristol or Perth. There is a category of 'Outstanding Conservation Area' awarded by a national body, the Historic Buildings Council, but this is more a response to requests for financial help in restoring historic buildings than an attempt to set up a national definition; nonetheless almost every CBA town centre is an Outstanding Conservation Area.

The urban villages

The population frequency distribution given earlier gives the impression that the smaller the population of a place the more likely it is to appear on the CBA list, but there is a point when a place is not so much a historic town as a historic village with some urban characteristics—what I call an 'urban village'.

Visually urban villages are 'urban' in that the houses are built in a continuous frontage (with long thin burgage plots behind) along the streets, in contrast to a village with detached cottages and front gardens. Though many consist basically of one long street, others have intricate street patterns, usually spreading out from a central market space, often still with an island town or market hall. Functionally these places are villages now, being all parishes before the 1968 re-organisation, and have few shops and few of the functions of a town.

To me a historic town must not only be historic but a town, and not a town in historic times but a town in the 1980s, with the market, shopping and administrative functions of a town rather than a village—however much this may cause problems of town centre development and parking. It is the bustle and thriving character of these market towns, the fact that country people and farmers come in to shop, that is an essential element in my picture of a historic town and my enjoyment of one. So the majority of the urban villages are not covered in the Gazetteer. They are often so overwhelmed with tourists seeking cream teas that I prefer to concentrate on the larger places—the small market towns, that are surprisingly little known and appreciated.

The places on the CBA list above 40,000

Whereas one can generalise about the bulk of the CBA list, it is increasingly difficult as one moves up the population scale with the 41 CBA towns over 40,000. The larger the town, the more remarkable its survival from the pressures of growth, and the more necessary an individual explanation for each town.

Twenty-eight form a long tail to the frequency distribution:

1971 population

Tamworth, Weymouth, Perth, Scarborough, Tunbridge Wells	40,000 +
Leamington Spa, Hereford, Ayr, Lancaster, Dunfermline	45,000 +
Great Yarmouth, St Albans	50,000 +
Rochester, Shrewsbury, Mansfield	55,000 +
Chester, Barrow-in-Furness	60,000 +

Greenock   65,000 +
Peterborough, Carlisle, Hove, Worcester, Lincoln,
    Cheltenham   70,000 +
Colchester   75,000 +
Bath   80,000 +
Exeter excluding Topsham, Gloucester   90,000 +

And finally 13 CBA towns I call historic cities: Cambridge 98,840; York 104,782; Oxford 108,805; Norwich 122,083; Ipswich 123,312; Northampton 126,642; Brighton 161,351 (with Hove 234,437); Aberdeen 182,071; Southampton 215,118; Newcastle-upon-Tyne 222,209; a jump to Nottingham 300,630; a big jump to Edinburgh and Leith 453,584; and a huge jump to the biggest of all, Glasgow 897,483.

My disagreements with the CBA list

Readers may be surprised at the inclusion of Mansfield and of Barrow-in-Furness, which was created in the 1860s. In Mansfield (and Belper) the CBA seems to be introducing a new type—the early-industrial town. With my interest in canals, I much enjoy the workers' terraces, flagstones and cobbles of the usually hilly Pennine early-industrial towns; but if the CBA includes any, it should include finer examples such as Macclesfield and Halifax.

Some of the CBA's other selections seem inexplicable to me now; but as the CBA drew up the list in 1965 and I've been exploring the towns since 1976, this may be because the pace of urban redevelopment has been so destructive in the intervening dozen years that the CBA would not now include them either—as with Tamworth, Peterborough and Northampton, all sacked by the planners for recent forced high growth.

I have not only *excluded* places for the Gazetteer, I have *added* some of my own, giving 6″ maps to Aberaeron, Alnwick, Frome and Petworth. The average population of the towns given 6″ maps is 17,033.

The large towns on the CBA list

Having discussed whether certain places are too *small* to be historic towns, let us now look at the other end of the scale and see whether some are not too *large*. Here the highest category of urban status before 1968 is relevant—whether a town was a County Borough (or in Scotland a County of City).

During the heady days of high growth, almost all towns that were County Boroughs, because they had the powers to do so, went in for huge Comprehensive Redevelopment schemes, ripping down large parts of their historic centres, and blitzing through great new urban roads against the grain of the historic street pattern and plan. These towns thought of themselves primarily as regional shopping and office centres rather than historic towns. They aped the Inner Ring Roads of big cities like Birmingham and went for the supposed benefits of eliminating small 'non-conforming' industries and housing from the city centres; only in the late 1970s did they begin to realise their mistakes, having acquired the big city's almost insoluble problems as well.

With these factors and the earlier frequency distribution in mind, it could be argued that, however unique its history or extensive its historic buildings and streets today, simply by being large, no large town can be a 'historic' town — that 'large historic town' like 'Victorian historic town' is a contradiction in terms. Certainly exploring them is a different experience from the typical much smaller historic town, part of the pleasure being the contrast between the new shops and offices, and the historic streets, with the surprise and incongruity of finding so much of historic value left.

One could argue that one is now simply talking about historic areas within our big cities, that it is wrong for the CBA to list Glasgow, Greenock, Nottingham and Southampton and not Leicester, Coventry and, most controversially, Bristol which has six Outstanding Conservation Areas within its central area. All I can say is that I do find, despite new urban roads, an overall unity and continuity of the historic street pattern in the few big cities the CBA does choose, a regular woven fabric rather than a few patches of cloth, that I do not find in the centre of Bristol or Leicester as a whole, nor Coventry where the city planners, setting out in the 1940s and 1950s to be a pioneering example of the Brave New Socialist World, deliberately destroyed the historic street pattern for their new pedestrian shopping precinct. So I agree with the CBA's choice — except Northampton which only comes into the big league because of its recent destructive growth — but would suggest a new category, 'historic city':

York and Norwich: two of the great medieval cities of Europe; though large towns now, they were exceptionally large in the Middle Ages, so have grown relatively little since — the walls of York being $2\frac{3}{4}$ miles round, of Norwich $2\frac{1}{4}$.

Ipswich: surprisingly similar to Norwich and undervalued.

Bath: a unique C18 resort extension of London — 'London in the country'.

Brighton and Hove: an early C19 'London by the Sea', similarly metropolitan in character.

Oxford and Cambridge: surviving because the colleges owned most of the land and forced the industries and growth to the East (making Oxford the Latin Quarter of Cowley).

Newcastle-upon-Tyne and Aberdeen: because of the outstanding quality of their early C19 town centre redevelopments.

Nottingham: with an unusually extensive historic core from the Anglian burh round St Mary's to the Norman borough beneath the castle.

Southampton: with two excellent historic areas—the walled medieval port, like a historic site or open-air museum; and the Regency resort areas facing or near the fine inland commons.

Edinburgh & Leith: its New Town claimed as the largest planned development in the world, Edinburgh merits (along with Dublin) another category, 'historic capital'.

Glasgow: twice the size of Edinburgh, with a handsome West End and opulent Victorian buildings, as has **Greenock**. Both are substantially underrated.

The Scottish and Welsh towns have the characteristics of English Towns of twice the population, which is why the smallest places in the Gazetteer are in Scotland and Wales and have not been excluded as being urban villages. So Greenock is excluded as a historic city; and one should expect new urban roads and blight in Ayr, Dunfermline and Perth, and, in towns of less than 40,000, at Inverness, Stirling, Dumfries and Aberystwyth.

Despite the many merits of the historic cities, I do not deal with them in the Gazetteer, because they are really a different animal, and for the practical considerations that the 6″ maps of their historic cores would be too big for the pages of this book, and the perambulations too long and extensive. Oxford, Cambridge and Bath are not very extensive, but they are so well covered already they are excluded. Finally I exclude from the Gazetteer, rather arbitrarily perhaps, three towns on the margin between historic town and historic city:

Cheltenham: its fine stone and stucco Regency developments are overwhelming in extent and rival in scale the two mile seafront of Brighton and Hove.

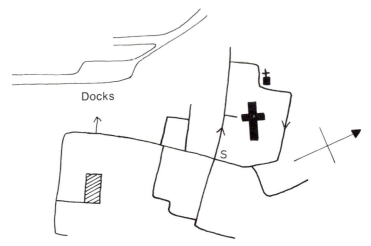

Docks

Gloucester: particularly nastily redeveloped. Start at The Cross. Good loop along best street, Westgate, round cathedral along Pitt Street, back along Northgate Street. Then Southgate Street with Greyfriars behind to the left, Blackfriars to the right (three grand c18 houses near Shire Hall), out to two good early c19 areas—on left villas and terraces of Brunswick Square and facing gardens, on right superb warehouses and textures of canal and docks.

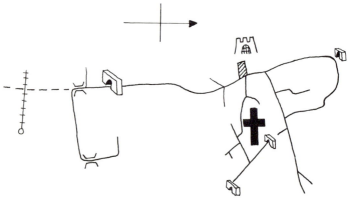

Lincoln: feels like a large Northern industrial city and has less historic town to explore than Boston or Stamford. Explore the High Town from Castle Hill, the best space: to Newport Arch; round Roman wall to Eastgate and out beyond fork; through Exchequer Gate to the cathedral and the lanes and buildings along its southern side. Then a mile down the spine of the town to s: delightful Steep Hill, through Stonebow, over medieval High Bridge with houses, across two level crossings to the Norman guild buildings next to St Peter-at-Gowts Saxon tower.

2 Historical Aspects

It is obviously impossible to cover here the history of all British historic towns. So all I attempt is a few comments, emphasising primarily how some knowledge of a town's history adds to the pleasures of walking round and exploring it, aspects included in Aston and Bond's *The Landscape of Towns* (1976), and to a lesser extent, in Colin Platt's *The English Medieval Town* (1976). Both books have useful bibliographies.

By contrast with today, Britain was in medieval times one of the least urbanised countries in Europe, its towns (outside London) being smaller than those of the Low Countries, North Italy and France. 'The population of this island does not appear to me to bear any proportion to her fertility and riches,' wrote an Italian visitor about 1500, when there were an estimated $2\frac{1}{2}$ to 3 million people in England—and 8 million sheep! One could probably consider the Belgic tribal capitals at Colchester and Winchester as towns; but urban life really dated from the Romans who invaded a century later, and founded many military forts or camps (hence *castra*, the name ending of -chester, -cester, -eter), many of which grew into towns.

What happened in the Anglo-Saxon invasions and the Dark Ages is still being debated. Some places were abandoned and never became towns again; some probably lay ruined and deserted for some time; while those with walls, like London, Canterbury, Lincoln and York, may have survived in continuous occupation, though probably in no sense as towns. So we owe to the Romans the *sites* of a number of today's towns, showing that the military corps that chose them had a keen eye for geographical position and economic potential, and sometimes the line of their walls, especially when re-used in Saxon and medieval times, and the line of the main internal cross-streets between the gates, as at Chichester. Usually the Saxon or later street plan was completely different even if also to a grid, as shown in excavations at Winchester and Leicester.

Initially ignoring or possibly even destroying towns rather than creating them, it was probably not until the C9 that the Angles and Saxons had settlements one could call towns—the 'ceaster' on Roman sites, the 'port' a commercial centre with market rights (often near the sea, as Bridport, but often inland as Langport), and the fortified place, the 'burh'. The creation of towns was stimulated by later invaders, the Danes, who administered their conquered territory, the Danelaw from York, Nottingham,

Lincoln, Leicester, Stamford and Derby. The Saxons, particularly Alfred from Wessex, responded by establishing a number of 'burhs', usually surrounded by earth and timber defences. Some never became commercially successful, but a number became market towns and/or the centre of newly formed shires. In some larger 'burhs' not too confined by their sites, a grid of streets was laid out within the defences (as at Wareham and Wallingford), and also within the Roman defences of Winchester, Chichester, Dorchester (Dorset), Exeter, Bath and Gloucester.

Ninth and tenth century monastic reforms led to larger and more elaborate abbeys, and indirectly to the creation, often actively promoted, of abbey towns: at Ely, Abingdon, Evesham, Pershore, Glastonbury, and St Albans—where Abbot Wulsin about 950 diverted Watling Street to the abbey gates and laid out a triangular market place, offering free timber to potential traders. Parallel with this was the moving of a number of bishop's sees between 1050 and 1101, from small settlements to larger defended settlements that were obviously important towns: from Dorchester-on-Thames to Lincoln; Lichfield to Chester and then to Coventry; Wells to Bath; Sherborne to Old Sarum; Selsey to Chichester; Crediton to Exeter; and from North Elmham to Thetford and then to Norwich.

So the Saxon (and Danish) contribution to the appearance of our towns today was, like the Roman, a number of new *sites*; and unlike them, important elements in today's street plan—often the basic medieval plan when it has survived till today. Many Saxon towns have continued to flourish right up to the present day, which gives one a remarkable feeling of *continuity*, as one explores these towns today—the realisation as one picks one's way through the market stalls near St Albans' clock tower, that trading like this has been carried on here for over a thousand years.

Then came the Norman Conquest, the Domesday survey of the spoils in 1086, and the emergence of a new type, the castle town. The Saxon burh was designed as a defence for the whole population, but the Norman castle (initially at least) was an alien element, the refuge of a Norman feudal lord against an enslaved and hostile Saxon population. The lords at Ludlow and Bridgnorth granted market rights and laid out the street plan; but there was probably a delay of a century or so before the settlements outside the castle gates became economically thriving towns, started to generate wealth and trade or offer services not connected with the castle household. However, many castle towns went on to become very prosperous, as symbolised by the magnificent largely c15 cruciform parish church at Ludlow (whose central tower competes with the castle on the skyline), paid for by burgesses wealthy from the cloth trade—showing again, as with the Romans, that strategic sites often turn out to be economically sound as well.

The Normans established castles and the first towns on the Welsh Marches; also in Wales, particularly along the South coast with Cardiff, Swansea, Abergavenny, Chepstow, Haverfordwest, Monmouth and Pembroke. Tenby seems to have been a Flemish trading settlement in the early C12, before acquiring its castle. Cowbridge—with C13/early C14 town walls but no castle—is given a CBA date as 'urban' of '1090–1262', a salutary reminder of how little evidence there often is.

It was in the C12 that the first towns appeared in Scotland, directly or indirectly established by kings (particularly David I, 1124–1153) influenced by what was happening in England. Edinburgh and Stirling grew up under the shadow of royal castles; Arbroath and Jedburgh of newly-founded abbeys; Glasgow, Brechin and St Andrews of founded or refounded cathedrals. However, St Andrews was also made a Royal Burgh in 1140, showing a trading function as well; and though some acquired abbeys and/or castles later, most of the other Scottish historic towns listed were founded for commercial reasons.

Besides establishing castles on strategic new sites, the Normans wanted to control the important existing towns; so they built new castles next to these or often into the existing urban fabric, demolishing 166 houses at Lincoln and 51 at Shrewsbury, and affecting the town plans of Oxford and Colchester.

Domesday is notoriously unreliable on towns; a place described as having 'burgesses' was probably a town, but many known towns of the time are not mentioned at all. London, Norwich, York, Lincoln, Winchester are the only towns given more than a thousand burgesses and Bristol's revenue was estimated as high. Deducing actual populations is anybody's guess, but London, the largest, was probably of the order of 20,000, with the others between 10,000 and 5000; in an England of, say, a million people (much the same as in Roman times) about 100,000 were in towns. Most of those towns were a 'mere collection of huts and houses surrounded by an earthen bank' (Hoskins).

Planned towns

From Domesday till 1345 the population of England increased to about four million, and towns shared in this growth.

As a result presumably of the irregular street plans and frontages of most historic towns, it was thought until recently that most towns grew 'organically' in a seemingly 'natural' progress—from being a hamlet, to a village, and finally a town, and that this depended on geographical and economic factors, such as being on a navigable river, on trade routes between two more important towns or at the junction of two river valleys. However the recent boom in urban archaeology and a number of studies of particular towns are emphasising the importance of human factors and especially the attitude and policies of the local landowner—from local squires, barons once they ventured outside their castles, abbots, bishops, up to the king. More and more it now seems that a town needed two factors to be successful: 'natural' geographical and economic advantages allied with strenuous efforts by local landowners, the 'capitalist developers'.

The extent of those efforts depended largely on the enthusiasm and wealth of the 'developer'. The minimum risk was incurred by giving market rights, perhaps laying out a market place and diverting main roads through it and offering inducements to traders such as free building materials and waiting to see what happened. If the settlement grew, the landowner released further land, but often with no attempt to lay out new streets or burgage plots, so the town's development might in retrospect look 'organic'.

However, many landowners went on to a second stage: of grafting on to an existing growing town a grid of 'new' streets and burgage plots, often now called Newtown or Newlands. As successive PhD dissertations reveal new C12 or C13 quarters in almost every historic town studied in detail, one now looks suspiciously at any plan configuration of streets, lanes or ends of burgage plots that makes anything like a rectangle or grid.

Finally the project of laying out a complete new town, usually to a grid: this was an enterprise of such scale it could only be done by the biggest landowners, culminating in the activities of Edward I. Notable Norman grid towns are the fine hill town of Ludlow, already mentioned as a castle town, and two abbey towns laid out the opposite side of the abbey from previous Saxon towns—Peterborough and Bury St Edmunds. The Bishop of Worcester laid out Stratford-upon-Avon in 1197 to a grid at an angle, defined by Bridge Street, the Roman road from the ford (hence the name Stratford) to Alcester; the burgage plots were 12 perches deep with a $3\frac{1}{2}$ perch frontage (1 perch = $5\frac{1}{2}$ yards). Salisbury (New Sarum) was laid out by the bishop in the 1220s with a more rectilinear grid of 'chequers', 7 perches by 3. Then Edward I established a number of military new towns (*bastides*) in North Wales which he hoped would also be commercially successful, following precedents in France.

While towns needed human intervention to back up natural geographical factors, it was equally necessary for the ambitious schemes of Edward I or anyone else to be supported by geographical and economic advantages if they were to succeed. There were many cases of ambitiously planted new towns failing due to geographical factors. Edward I's New Winchelsea, laid out on a site of 150 acres, with the most spacious grid of all, is now, due to silting up of the harbour and repeated sackings by the French, not a town today, nor visually even a village but a sort of Hampstead Garden Suburb with cellars. The map (of 1855) shows Hedon, a Humberside port laid out in 1138, its grid of streets now petering out in the marshes, with only its magnificent cruciform church as a reminder of its former importance. Hedon silted up and was replaced by Wyke-upon-Hull, created by the nearby Cistercian abbey of Meaux in the late C12 (using the river

Hull to scour out the channel?) which became Kingston-upon-Hull when Edward I bought it in 1293. Hoskins picks out another: 'On the southern shore of Poole Bay in Dorset, directly opposite the ancient port of Poole, is the site of a completely still-born royal town—Nova Villa. King Edward I, that great town-planner, gave it a charter in 1286, conferring upon it all the liberties and privileges of the City of London. A site was chosen, two town-planners appointed (one of them a parson), the town marked out on the ground: but all in vain. Nothing happened. In Elizabethan days, three hundred years later, the solitary farm of Newton, standing upon the heath that petered out in the muddy flats of the bay, alone marked the site of Edward I's "New Town" '.

In retrospect, remembering our earlier 'model' of historic towns a reasonable distance apart, each with its catchment area, it was a mistake for Nova Villa to try and compete with Poole.

Such failures were not only due to geographical factors such as channels silting up, but to a sudden decline in the total population. In 1349 came the first outbreak of the Black Death which killed between a third and a half of the entire population and wiped out certain settlements almost completely. The population of England in 1500 was still well below what it was in 1349.

Parish churches

The most spectacular indication of the wealth and importance of many historic towns is the size and splendour of their parish churches. First come the five English parish churches over 20,000 square feet in area: St Nicholas, Great Yarmouth; the great C14 brick church of Holy Trinity at Hull; two that later became parish-church cathedrals—St Nicholas at Newcastle-upon-Tyne, and St Michael at Coventry, burnt out in 1940, its shell an impressive forecourt to Basil Spence's new cathedral. And most spectacular of all, St Botolph's, with a Decorated interior and its 272-foot steeple 'the Stump', at Boston. To these I would add: St Lawrence at Ludlow; St Mary Redcliffe at Bristol; Grantham; Louth—its 295 ft steeple rivalling Boston Stump; Nottingham and Newark; the great Cotswold wool churches and that at Cirencester, almost as wide and tall as it is long; the two churches at King's Lynn; Ashbourne; the early C16 church at Newbury paid for by John Smallwood, a wealthy cloth merchant; in Wales Haverfordwest, Tenby and Conway; and in Scotland, the 'burgh kirks' of Haddington, Linlithgow, Stirling, Perth, St Andrews, and St Giles at Edinburgh.

One should distinguish parish churches from cathedral-type

churches (like the abbey churches at Leominster, Malmesbury, Pershore, Shrewsbury, Tewkesbury and Wymondham) which may be associated with the history of the town but which are not a symbol or reflection of the subsequent wealth of the town. So at Beverley, the Minster is not so good an indicator of the subsequent wealth of the medieval town as is the spacious St Mary's near the Market Place. Collegiate churches are more difficult to split into these categories—as at Tamworth, Stratford-upon-Avon or Lancaster, but those at Warwick and Arundel seem to owe more to the wealth and power of their feudal barons than the wealth of the towns.

One should not assume that because certain important historic towns have not been mentioned as having spectacular parish churches they were not wealthy or did not believe in building churches. Certain towns had a large number of churches, rather than their resources being concentrated into just one church (often dedicated to the all-purpose guild of Holy Trinity). Within their walls, the City of London had 97 medieval parish churches, Norwich 56 (with St Peter Mancroft nonetheless unusually large), York 39 (or 40?), Lincoln 34, Exeter 16, Ipswich 15, Oxford and Wallingford 13, with more churches in the extramural suburbs.

The position and status of the church often indicates a town being planted or planned: when the parish church is some distance from the town centre, as at Stratford-upon-Avon where it is down the original village street still called Old Town, and at Brackley and Thame; or where the central church has no graveyard and was or still is a chapel-at-ease (ie with no burial rights) to a parish church elsewhere—as at Henley-in-Arden (to Beaudesert $\frac{1}{4}$ mile E), Bewdley (to Ribbesford), Market Harborough (to Great Bowden), and as the huge Holy Trinity at Kingston-upon-Hull was until 1661. The names of the last two indicate their planted origins; and the impressive St Nicholas King's Lynn, still a chapel-at-ease, together with the second (Tuesday) market place was part of the 'Nova Terra' laid out north of the earlier town in 1150–70.

Names and associations

Many town names indicate their planted or planned origins: obviously, as in Newcastle, Newmarket, Newport and the abbey towns of St Albans, Peterborough, Bury St Edmunds; less obviously in Baldock coming from Baldac, the old French name for Baghdad, indicating its late C12 foundation by the Knights Templar. Historic street names also indicate new or planned elements within towns, such as New Street or Newlands as well as historical elements such as Friars Street or topographically useful ones—Church Street leading to the church etc. Unfortunately the Victorians often changed street names to make them more 'respectable' so one should look out, on buildings at street corners and on old maps, for the former names. At Stratford, Ely Street was formerly Swine Street (because a pig market was held in the street), and Windsor Street formerly Hell Lane; and at Banbury interesting speculation is occasioned by one of the main streets changing its name (as early as 1410) from Gropecunt Lane to Parsons Lane. The actual names, often cast-iron in a Baskerville type fixed to corner buildings, are usually visually attractive; whereas modern names, typographically designed in a faceless style to be seen at night at 30 mph, are either genteel Laburnum Grove, Acacia Avenue etc, or reveal their concrete dual-carriageway character with names like Corporation Street, Churchill or Maid Marian (Nottingham) Way.

Many buildings and walls have plates fixed to them indicating the site of a town gate or monastic house, or plaques that famous people lived or worked there. I personally find this type of historical association less poignant or evocative than many people do, and for this to add to my architectural appreciation of the actual building I need the building to be contemporary with the great man; so a plaque that 'this Inner Ring Road is on the site of a house lived in by . . .' does not turn me on. Stratford-upon-Avon, despite its commercialisation, does evoke Shakespeare to me because large parts of the town were burnt down and rebuilt in Shakespeare's time, in the 1590s; one can almost imagine him jostling with the Japanese in the streets; so contrary to the opinion of the director of the Shakespeare Birthplace Trust, I think the general architectural character of Stratford most important to the Shakespeare industry; if Shakespeare had been born in Slough ('come friendly bombs and fall on Slough'—Betjeman), I do not believe there would be a similar Shakespeare industry in Slough. Similarly Lichfield, being a comfortable Georgian city with other associations (Elias Ashmole, David Garrick, Erasmus Darwin) does convey something of Dr Johnson as well as having his birthplace; but it is Laugharne's situation and its small-town character, rather than its architecture, that reminds me it was Dylan Thomas's Llareggub.

The elements of the plan

The raw material is the street plan, to be studied and enjoyed both from maps and from the varied frontages, street widths, curves, narrowings and long thin alleys encountered when actually exploring the town. The elements to be looked for have been mentioned already, and used in our definition of a historic town. In general one can usually distinguish planned towns or parts of towns by their straightness and grid plans. The older strategic roads cross the grid at various angles, as in Leamington. Then at the town centre, and even now the best general starting point for the exploration of a historic town, there is usually an open space laid out as the market place. Usually rectangular in shape, it is occasionally a widening at the junction of several roads or triangular to reflect its back-to-the-wall origins as at St Albans (to the abbey) and Taunton (to the Norman castle). Many market towns had basically only one long wide street in which markets and fairs took place—such as at Marlborough and Thame and Ludlow's Broad, Mill and High Streets, while some places simply had a river or sea front. Load Street, Bewdley was built especially wide as a market place, for loading produce at its quays on the river Severn.

Almost all towns, whether their plans are complex or simple, single streets or a grid, have, in their property boundaries, long narrow burgage plots running back from the main streets. The houses run in a continuous frontage along the streets, and even if the present buildings are mixed architecturally or relatively recent, there is usually a characteristic burgage plot width and frontage length that forms the visual module of the street, giving the historic street scene a variety of human scale, and important vertical lines, shadows and changes of plane, between one plot and the next. When a modern developer purchases several of these burgage plots and clears the site, if the frontage length of the new building is not broken down into the characteristic module (and indeed height) of the street, it can spoil the appearance of the whole street; much bad infill of this type was built in historic high streets in the 1950s, but recently planning authorities have shown a greater understanding of this point and 1960s and 1970s infill was generally scaled down.

The original plot dimensions varied but Alnwick's 28′ and 32′ frontages seem fairly typical, with subdivision of plots occurring quite early. Interesting deductions about the phases in the growth of a town, or which were its chief streets, can be attempted by looking at what happened at corners or noting where burgage plots do not run back at right angles to the frontage of the street. At a corner, a street with a burgage plot side wall is presumably less important (or later) than that with the short built-up frontage; Stratford and Thame's angled plots indicate older important roads; while at Tewkesbury, confined by the Severn flood plain to W and S and abbey lands to E, and the best town in Britain to explore burgage plots, those on the E side of the High Street turn (once back beyond the actual buildings on the frontage) to run parallel to Barton Street, probably an old road developed later.

On the other side of Tewkesbury's High Street the burgage plots run right back to the Avon, as they do back to the river or seafront that formed the basis of the prosperity of many historic towns, such as those S of the High Street at Ware. Here one can imagine the life of the merchant in the C16 and C17 as described by W G Hoskins:

> On the main street the merchant had his tiny shop and behind that were the kitchen and the buttery; the other living rooms were piled up above ... At the back door, so to speak, the merchant's ships unloaded straight into his warehouses, and at the front door, he was selling pennyworths of goods to retail customers. In between, he carried on the wholesale business that was the mainstay of his livelihood [and] covered the whole range of trading, from importer to retail shopkeeper.

The streets of early medieval towns, whether planned or organic, were usually spacious and wide, and the burgage plots large, with considerable gardens behind. In fact the plots are so long at such one-street towns as Chipping Campden and Thame (650 to 700') that one imagines a transition between urban and rural life, with the owners half engaged on agriculture and growing their own food at the back, and half selling goods or services at their shops at the front.

However, during the course of the Middle Ages and indeed right up to the middle of the C19, burgage plot frontages were often halved or even quartered and the plots filled in with long ranges of buildings, sometimes 'courts' with housing for the poor, sometimes warehousing and industrial uses, over the former gardens, with alleys for access. This is why one can explore nearly all Tewkesbury's burgage plots along the alleys. Such infilling led to much overcrowding and sub-standard housing, and many of the courts have been demolished or cleared out in the last hundred years, often necessarily to improve the quality and attractiveness of the houses along the street. Nonetheless examples survive to be explored in nearly every historic town; historic inns are the best starting points, for they often still have deep courtyards or long ranges of buildings and are accessible to the public.

It was not only the burgage plots that became infilled later, but the broad main street and the market place itself. The market stalls often became solidified as permanent dwellings, encroaching on the streets from the sides, or else lines of stalls became infill islands, with the lord or municipality often leading the way—as with the superb medieval market crosses at Chichester, Malmesbury and Salisbury and with so many town or market halls, now freestanding buildings on an island, originally open at ground floor to shelter the stallholders, with a room above for the town council to meet and surmounted with a coat of arms, clock or cupola. So historic streets were often much wider than they are today, and many market places were of much greater extent. At Ludlow for instance, four parallel lanes and streets lead to the top of the town into what appear to be two little squares on either side of the Victorian redbrick Market Hall; but in fact the buildings between the four streets and the island Market Hall are all later encroachments in the original broad High Street and the little squares are the only places where the street is its original width. Hitchin's market place originally went right up to Tilehouse Street and The Priory, occupying all the land between Sun Street and High Street; and Bury St Edmunds' original market place now has two long island rows plus three fine island public buildings.

The town wall and defences

Finally the feature that defines the medieval core of many historic towns, the town wall. Though most people, including myself, talk of a 'wall', and of the towns as 'walled', the type of defences varied and was often modified over the centuries. Even in medieval times they were not always continuous walls of stone, but sometimes only ditches and embankments, presumably originally surmounted by a timber stockade. Though the Gazetteer map of Sandwich refers to 'Town Wall', the existing walk is along an embankment with a ditch, and a complete wall may never have been built.

Most important Roman towns were walled in stone, and the complete line (and even some of the masonry) was re-used in the medieval walls of Bath, Chichester, Colchester and Exeter—and partly at Chester, Gloucester and Rochester. The Saxon and Danish burh defences were usually earth banks, and were modified and re-used in part of the medieval walls at Hereford and Nottingham, which incorporated market place areas developed outside the original burhs. Towns not refortified after the Conquest included: Dorchester with its Roman and Wallingford and Wareham with their Saxon earth defences almost complete; and Buckingham, Derby, Hertford, Maldon, Malmesbury and Thetford (a site s of the river and of the later medieval town).

The whole question of town defences is being actively researched at the moment; but Hilary Turner calculated in 1970 that in England and Wales of 249 towns in possession of charters by 1520, 108 were walled—of which 84 still had some remains today. While certain towns had walls designed against attack by foreign armies, for most towns having a stone wall was not so much a military necessity as a status symbol of a town's wealth and importance—to defend the privileges of the guilds and merchants within the walls against the less privileged without.

So it is not surprising that most important medieval towns had stone walls, particularly those that acquired the unusual status of being counties in their own right, 'counties corporate', with the right to have their own sheriffs, an anticipation of the County Borough status introduced in 1888. This privilege was given by the king to a town for the loan of money or its support against local barons or rival factions for the throne. London got the status in the 1190s, then Bristol in 1373 breaking away from Gloucestershire, York in 1396, Newcastle-upon-Tyne 1400, Norwich 1404, Lincoln 1409, Kingston-upon-Hull 1440, Southampton 1447, Nottingham 1449, Coventry 1451 (its walls not finished until 1537), Canterbury 1461, Haverfordwest 1479, Gloucester 1482, Chester 1506 and Exeter in 1537; and Edinburgh had had sheriffs of its own since 1482. Then Lichfield became a county corporate in 1553—given by Queen Mary for its citizens' 'diligent industry and faithful service in the time of the rebellion in her behalf', but it only had earth defences, much weaker and later than the stone walls of the cathedral precinct; similarly the defences of town and abbey at St Albans. However the last three counties corporate all had medieval stone walls: Poole which got the status in 1568, Carmarthen 1604, ending with Worcester in 1622—in Stuart times, explaining perhaps its devotion to the Stuart cause, its walls being refortified and extended in the Civil War.

Again most of the towns appearing in W G Hoskins' ranking of the first 42 English provincial towns in 1334, 1377, 1523–7 (in *Local History in England*) had medieval stone walls, and fine parish churches as well. All the counties corporate appear high in the rankings. Of the others, listed at all three dates: Colchester, Hereford, King's Lynn (part of its circuit perhaps only a ditch), Leicester, Northampton, Oxford, Plymouth, Stamford, Winchester and Yarmouth were walled in stone; but Boston, Bury St Edmunds, Cambridge, Ipswich (parts in stone) and Salisbury had only earth defences besides their rivers; and at Reading the abbey was walled in stone, but the town was undefended until fortified in the Civil War.

Much of the purpose of town walls was to define 'rateable values', to take market tolls and to control people and goods passing through a town, as a means of excluding marauders and if necessary the plague. Since the burgage plots usually formed a continuous frontage along the streets, many of these policing functions could be achieved just by having gates—as at Glasgow, Tewkesbury, Bewdley and New Aberdeen. In fact one suspects that almost every town, even those generally considered completely undefended, had toll bars across the streets at the approaches to the town, which were made more permanent when marauders threatened.

How important are the 'town walls' in the townscape and environment of historic towns today? The most spectacular stretches surviving have already been mentioned on page 7, to which I would add considerable stretches at Chepstow, Colchester, Denbigh (the deserted town on the hill next to the castle), Exeter, Hereford, King's Lynn, Pembroke, Rye, Shrewsbury and Winchester.

But the walls do not have to be standing to have a crucial importance in the townscape. The roads that ran inside and/or outside the line often still survive, streets and lanes stop mysteriously, streets narrow where there used to be gates—all most easily seen from the plans, but environmentally defining the character and extent of the central core. Recently this has been emphasised in Canterbury, Hereford and Worcester, where new Inner Ring Roads have been built largely following the line of the walls—a more modern and nastier version of the tree-lined boulevards round the walls or along their line in many continental historic towns.

The maps in this book show, apart from existing stretches, the rest of the line at Totnes (with two gates) and the line where no wall remains at Barnstaple and at Aberystwyth; but it is difficult to deduce even the line of the well-documented wall at Haverfordwest. At Stamford, Broad Street and St Mary's Street with the bends of the old Great North Road mark the edge of the Danish burh (and streets s of the river in the medieval extramural suburb of St Martin's mark the Saxon burh) while Wharf Road (to SE), North Street and East Street mark the line of the medieval walls that took in a larger area including the castle and the market place. Great Yarmouth's map shows the line of the walls, but it is more notable for its unique shape and its famous 150 narrow lanes (the 'rows'), of which only a few have survived the air-raids in 1942.

Castle towns were half of them defended and half undefended.

If the interests of a castle and the castle town beside the gates were common, as they increasingly became once the Norman invaders had settled in, the inhabitants of a castle town could shelter if necessary within the castle walls. Similarly the inhabitants of a cathedral or abbey town could shelter within the cathedral or abbey precinct walls. But certain castle towns did acquire walls of their own, always later and less substantial than those of the castle, expressing perhaps the growing economic importance of the town's merchants. So Bridgnorth, Ludlow, Newark and Warwick eventually acquired stone walls, plus Launceston and Richmond with walls almost indistinguishable from the outer baileys of their castles (two gates remain at Richmond, one at Launceston); and Bridgwater, Tutbury and Taunton acquired earth town defences.

Devizes has an extraordinary plan of curving streets which was determined by the town taking over the outer area of the castle, the castle bailey; the whole town plan is centred on the castle (later a great house, not open to the public). First a town developed outside the bailey with a market place, one side having burgage plots backing onto the castle bailey wall, the other side backing onto a defensive ditch and bank whose line can still be clearly seen. Then the castle bailey was colonised, and the later streets and fine present market place were all developed within it.

Other types of town that tended not to be defended were towns founded by ecclesiastical patrons and 'planted' or planned towns. Whether towns were walled also varied geographically across the country. The only defended towns in the sw counties of Cornwall, Devon and Dorset were Barnstaple, Exeter, Launceston, Plymouth, Poole and Totnes.

In the South-east, the threat of incursions by the French caused considerable effort to be made, most spectacularly at Southampton, at Rye and Canterbury, at Lewes (quite a few remains) and even round the planned town of Winchelsea despite its enormous perimeter (later reduced).

Many towns in the North of England were fortified against the Scots and Border robbers, most notably Carlisle which was repeatedly beseiged, the Counties Corporate (see page 26), Alnwick, Durham and Scarborough—all walled in stone. Lancaster apparently repaired its Roman fortifications, Beverley constructed a bank and ditch plus gates, but despite a murage grant, little may have been done at Penrith where there are no remains.

Since they were for the most part an alien English element in hostile country, almost all towns in Wales were fortified with stone walls. The best remains have been mentioned. Beaumaris (NE of Church Street), Brecon, Hay-on-Wye (across Newport Street to

NE) and Montgomery have remains plus a clear line; but there is little left at Monmouth (except the fortified bridge) or Cardigan. Llanidloes has C13 grid plan and the line of its earth defences. But were any defences ever constructed (despite murage grants) at Crickhowell, Knighton or Ruthin, or ever intended at Welshpool?

Of Scottish towns, only Edinburgh, Perth and Stirling were surrounded by medieval stone walls. Earth banks were more common, as at Dumfries (not complete circuit), usually with stone gates ('ports') as at Inverness (line of King Street W of river, Academy and Ardconnel Streets E). Kirkcudbright had a system of tide-filled ditches, with traces in the line of some of its present streets; and several towns had a makeshift wall made up of the bottom of burgage plots—of turf either side of Elgin's High Street, of stone, as can be seen, at Haddington and St Andrews (s of West Port). Perth's medieval wall doesn't impress the CBA which classifies its defences, along with Dumfries, Elgin and Peebles, as 'insubstantial or late C18'. The remains of Peebles' wall of 1570–4 are certainly insubstantial compared with the amazing new-style anti-gunpowder bastions and ravelins of the same period at Berwick-on-Tweed, which survive almost complete and leave out a section of Edward I's earlier wall.

This raises the question of post-medieval town fortifications. Chester and Colchester were beseiged during the Civil War, damaging their walls, but Newark was fortified far outside its medieval walls. Naval and dockyard towns continued to be defended right up to the mid C19 fortifications under Palmerston, with additions in the Second World War. Of these the Gazetteer covers only Harwich, with C12 grid plan and walls (along Kings Quay Street, remains in St Nicholas' churchyard), which was refortified in 1588 against the Armada, and has the impressive Redoubt against Napoleon.

Though it is a fascinating exercise to try and find documentary and physical evidence that a historic town once had 'walls', and if so, to deduce where they ran, to prevent the reader wasting too much time poring over the wrong Gazetteer maps with this in mind, an attempt has been made to mention in this section all those towns illustrated by OS maps that are known to have had medieval town walls or defences. Post-medieval towns given Gazetteer maps will be mentioned shortly, and these obviously didn't have town walls—unless perhaps Melcombe, the fore-runner of Weymouth, which received a murage grant in 1338? So the remainder can be assumed *not* to have had town defences. Some questions still remain however, like Henley-on-Thames, not mentioned for any defences and with no remains, but described as 'walled' by Burn, the local historian in 1861, with walls mentioned in corporation deeds in 1397 and 1531. If you can find traces of town walls here or in any of the other towns with maps not mentioned as walled, then write about it and get a PhD.

Obviously towns with town walls had extramural suburbs outside the walls, and these may have existed before the walls were built. Generally these suburbs housed 'noxious' trades, as that which gave its name to Smith Street outside the East gate at Warwick; but some of the richest men in Warwick lived in the extramural suburb of Bridge End (as they do now). Certain towns extended their walls later to include favoured suburbs, and although most extramural suburbs tended to be poor and became industrialised later with not much to see today, my perambulations do occasionally take the reader across the Inner Ring Road—to Bridge End, Warwick or to the favoured suburb of St Dunstan's at Canterbury.

The one remaining plan element listed by the CBA, a bridge crossing and approaches, needs no comment. And the layout of monastic and cathedral precincts, castles, and the detailed architectural questions of the design and type of medieval houses—whether parallel or at right angles to the street, hall house, Wealden-type with recessed facades—are best left to architectural guides and the burst of recent books on vernacular and timberframe buildings.

The development of Ludlow

Having once identified the medieval plan elements, it is then interesting to try and work out the order in which they occurred—the various phases of a town's development.

Let us look at what we can deduce from architectural, topographical and documentary evidence on a famous historic town, Ludlow. The map opposite shows: a planned gridtown with a wide EW market street (with later encroachments as described on page 25) and broad Mill and Broad streets to S (with back lanes between them) plus the previous N–S routeway—the old A49, now by-passed, (14) (12) (17)—over ford near Ludford mill; the original Norman castle on its rock above the junction of the rivers Corve and Teme, with its gatehouse/keep and round chapel; its late C12 extension to S and E to form the outer bailey; the clear line of the C13 town walls—to beyond the routeway, with a corner behind (12); medieval development outside the walls—funnelling from E through Galdeford gate, N beyond (14) to crossing of the Corve, S to Ludford bridge. By contrast there is the apparent decay of lower Mill Street and to W where a puzzling N–S

strip of property between (3) and (6) indicates a *third* planned N–S street, 'Christ Croft', whose top was destroyed for the castle bailey. So I used to assume the decay of this street occurred *because* of the extension of the castle, and that of the planned town S of the walls *because* it was outside the walls; and that medieval extramural suburbs developed much later—one of them being towards the present C15 Ludford bridge.

But I now (1980) learn from the Ludlow Historical Research Group that much of this is wrong or non-proven. For the C12 planned gridtown was 'burgaged' for a considerable distance—S to river, N and E to edge of map. What I thought was 'decay' was more probably the outlying plots not being taken up and settled in the first place (many were later given to religious houses); and a confirmatory charter of 1221 refers to a Ludford bridge. So the present C15 bridge is not the first, and lower Broad Street was not an extramural suburb to connect with it. Both the 'decay' and Ludford bridge were there well before the town walls were started in 1233. The walls seem, near Corve gate (12), to have been built through existing properties.

The Group also deduce, from N–S burgage plots along S side of the wide market street from the corner with Mill Street but stopping short of Broad Street (not clear on this map), a two-stage market place; they point out a N–S strip E of Broad Street, NNW from (23), indicating a second N–S planned street that became redundant; but they insist that both were not main streets but back access lanes—like the third, the existing Raven Lane. Faced with Raven Lane being so much narrower than the other two, and the fact that Christ Croft became redundant in an outlying area whilst the lane E of Broad Street became redundant in an area of high commercial pressures, I hazard the guess that Raven Lane is narrow because it was driven through earlier market place plots, before the grid plan was laid out; and that the other two back lanes became redundant because the land at their N ends became more valuable as frontage than the lanes as back access—perhaps about 1270 when the first of the infill rows and islands is recorded.

So at the present (1980) state of research, Ludlow's various stages seem to have been:

1. N–S routeway
2. Norman castle (1084–94) sited strategically on rock
3. Setting out (1100s) of first stage of wide market street to E
4. Laying out (C12) of large planned grid town with 33 ft burgage frontages, including:
    a extension of wide market street E to Bullring
    b broad Mill and Broad Streets to S
       plus three N–S back lanes
    c existing N–S routeway and routes in from E
5. Outlying plots not taken up and settled, so many were given to religious houses later
6. Late C12 extension of castle
7. Two of N–S back lanes become redundant
8. First Ludford bridge (late C12)
9. Construction of town walls 1233–1304, gates by 1270
10. Infilling of broad market street with rows and islands
11. First Dinham bridge (4)—medieval, C14 or C15?

What were the phases of development of other historic towns? How similar were they to Ludlow?

The post-medieval period

We have two periods when many historic towns were established, the Saxon, and the period from 1100 to 1350 when many boroughs were established or given market rights; the medieval towns which form the bulk of British historic towns, and whose plan elements we have just been looking at, were the successes from these phases of town development.

The late medieval period, and the C16 and C17, were less a period for establishing new settlements (except perhaps dockyard and military towns like Chatham and Tilbury) than for three processes occurring within existing towns:

1. The abandonment of the town walls or defences and the further development of extramural suburbs.
2. More significantly the infilling of the long burgage plots and of wide market streets.
3. The construction, whether along the street or down the alleys to the burgage plots, of most of the timberframe houses we see surviving today.

The process of infilling went on till about 1840; in Georgian times the alleys and courts and island town halls were usually constructed of brick, or stone if plentiful and cheap.

This is also, of course, the period when many towns began to become industrialised, often along these same alleys and courts, and though they were all well established in medieval times, it is primarily as C17 industrial towns that I think of the wool and cloth towns of Bradford-on-Avon and Frome, the salt town of Nantwich and the C18 silk and cotton town of Congleton.

It is along the coast in the late C17 that we get the next new burst of towns. Topsham emerges as the chief port of the River Exe; Pennycomequick on the Fal estuary (defended by two Henry VIII castles) was given a charter and made Falmouth by Charles II in 1660–1 after which its main Church Street was developed. Deal acquired three new streets parallel to the coast (no harbour: boats were, and are, pulled up the beach). Sir John Lowther established the grid seaport of Whitehaven, later in the C18 to rival Liverpool and Newcastle.

Inland England had its new ports too. In the late C18 James Brindley's decision to bring the Staffordshire & Worcestershire canal down the Stour valley to the Severn led to the unique canal transport town of Stourport, which took the river trade away from neighbouring Bewdley.

The greatest boom came later, in the late C18 and early C19, with the coastline being regarded not so much as a commercial asset for trade as an amenity beneficial to health, with the development of the Seaside Resort.

Resort towns, however, started not along the coast but inland, with the spa town where people of wealth and leisure went to 'take the waters'. Bath and Buxton originated as Roman spas; but the movement started when Henrietta Maria and her entire court camped near the springs of Tunbridge Wells in 1630 (its church, like that of Falmouth, is dedicated to King Charles the Martyr). The Walks (later the Parade, now the Pantiles) were laid out after 1687. Spas became fashionable with Bath, transformed in the first half of the c18 by 'Beau' Nash as Master of Ceremonies, by Ralph Allen providing the superb building stone, and by the architects and builders John Wood father and son. Then came Cheltenham, developed 1790–1830, and Leamington Spa 1806–1840, while in the 1780s the Duke of Devonshire gave Buxton its splendid Crescent and the Square.

The transition from spa to seaside resort is shown by Scarborough, where medicinal springs were found in the 1620s and seabathing became popular in the mid c18, causing the Georgian and Victorian developments N and s of the original medieval town near the castle. In Dorset Lyme Regis seems to have been a resort *near* the sea, enjoying the sea air without its breezes and storms, whereas Weymouth, patronised by George III in the 1790s, was the first resort *on* the sea, facing it architecturally with its impressive rows of redbrick bow windows. Then of course Brighton and Hove, Sidmouth, Ryde, Margate and Ramsgate, and in early Victorian times St Leonards grafted onto Hastings and in Wales the planned towns and ports of Tremadoc and Portmadoc, Aberaeron, and the carefully planned seaside resort of Llandudno.

The chief characteristics of all these resort historic towns are: their grid plans, varied with crescents, circuses and squares; formal architectural compositions, with terraces often of some length, usually with giant pilasters to mark the ends and sometimes also in the middle, with pediments of golden stone at Bath and Buxton and in the first phase at Cheltenham, initially brick elsewhere. Brick was later replaced almost everywhere by stucco facades which could be more easily repaired and repainted. Then Regency semi-detached houses came in, as in Leamington's delightful Lansdowne Circus; then Regency and early-Victorian villas, classical in style turning neo-Jacobean or neo-Gothic in the 1830s and 1840s. Broad tree-lined avenues and gardens both formal and informal make a general setting for the architecture.

Scotland has in Edinburgh the classic planned grid of the New Town; its architecture was always in stone, keeping to a classical style later than in England. Scotland has few spas and seaside resorts, but several c18 grid plantation towns to develop highland areas, such as the ports of Ardrossan, Fraserburgh and Peterhead, (New) Stonehaven on the coast and inland Fochabers, Grantown and the two grids at Keith.

Planned grid areas with terraces and squares not only sum up the second type of historic town, but form a second phase in many medieval historic towns as well. In almost every medieval town, timberframe houses were rebuilt or refronted in Georgian times; Warwick and Blandford Forum were largely rebuilt and their streets straightened after devastating fires in 1694 and 1731 respectively; many towns acquired completely new Georgian or Regency quarters. Almost every town on the coast transformed itself to some extent into a seaside resort, with good Georgian and Regency seaside architecture in Aberystwyth, Beaumaris, Tenby, Penzance, Southwold and Whitby—the seaside development of Yarmouth being later. Ashby-de-la-Zouch acquired a spa area.

We have now got to about 1840 and the end of 'historic' times, as defined in Chapter 1. A recurrent motif throughout has been planned towns and in particular the grid plan, from Roman times to Cheltenham and Brighton. So it is worth asking, in conclusion, why grid plan towns from these periods are attractive, whereas the grid plans of mid-Western America or Australia, and in Britain grid plan slums and Victorian bye-law housing in general are not. One reason is of course the architectural quality of the individual houses, of varied and local materials rather than Ruabon brick, mellowed by age and in general built for the well-to-do, whereas most Victorian grid-plan housing was built to low standards for the poorer classes. Another reason is the difference in the vistas down the streets. In American and Australian towns, usually on flat sites, the streets die disconsolately away into the horizon, whereas most of the Scottish grid-towns have afforested hillsides to close the vistas. Then the medieval grid towns have often acquired encroachments and islands to add variety, and the medieval planners staggered their street crossings (as at Baldock), perhaps to give protection from the wind (a lesson only recently relearnt by modern planners with their huge windswept precincts under tower blocks); and the resort towns usually have spacious avenues planted with trees—not found in slums and bye-law housing.

But the main reason is because Georgian and Regency architects and planners, inspired by the Woods at Bath, were well aware of the dangers of uniformity, used any small slopes of the site, incorporated older lanes as streets at angles to the grid, put in attractive buildings to close vistas, and varied the straight frontages with curved crescents and circuses, or with bow and bay windows. So however 'organically' the townscape of the earlier medieval historic towns may have arisen, or whatever the reason for their departures from strict grids, the townscape of the late historic towns, the spas and seaside resorts, was carefully contrived and organised for 'gentle folk and people of discrimination and taste' and we can still enjoy the results today. British architecture and planning have never been so successful since.

3 Introduction to the Gazetteer

It is hoped that readers find the first edition 6 inches to one mile Ordnance Survey maps as fascinating and interesting historical material, and as remarkable for their craftsmanship, as I do. The purpose of putting numbers on the maps, and the descriptions is:

1. to give the reader a recommended walk round the town—from (1) to (2) to (3);
2. to show him the extent of the town worth exploring and the best streets: some readers might be interested in exploring all the streets shown on the maps;
3. to mention some architectural features to look out for, though not necessarily all.

The numbers have been carefully placed over the historic os maps to cover as little as possible of historical or topographical interest. This means that a building is not always exactly (within 50 yards or so) where the number is placed on the map, and occasionally it is on the opposite side of the street. The text sometimes mentions a building, and gives it a number or asterisk on a map, because it is on a corner or marks the limit of the walk. It may not be the most important building on the stretch, so look out for good buildings not mentioned.

This gazetteer does not mention all the items of interest in a town, taking for granted the more usual tourist features such as cathedral, abbey, parish churches, castle, museum, assuming the reader has also one of the standard guidebooks. So the write-ups mention some features to look for, but by no means everything of interest.

Generally speaking the historic street plans of the towns given 6″ os maps have survived to make these maps accurate today, but occasionally new roads have been constructed since the date of the maps, islands of buildings removed, and more commonly, street names changed; the explorer should note and savour the differences. Similarly almost all the buildings mentioned in the text are listed Historic Buildings: they have a reasonable chance of having survived from when I did my surveys (1976–80) to when the reader explores the town, but the occasional building may have been demolished or changed beyond recognition.

When looking round:

1. Look out for interesting buildings other than those mentioned in the text.
2. As the original ground floors of many historic houses,

particularly in main shopping streets, have been spoilt by new plastic, steel and glass fascias and shopwindows, learn to look above ground level at the level of the eaves or at the corners.

3. To save space the descriptions do not in general include the names of streets or much historical information, so look out for street names, plaques about famous people associated with a building, or any other information displayed.

4. You will often have to cross the street to look at the top parts of a building from the opposite pavement; when exploring historic towns, one seems to be nearly always, at any particular moment, on the wrong side of the street. Don't sue me if you step backwards under a bus.

5. Because of the commercial pressures mentioned above, look out especially for the rare unspoilt medieval, Georgian or Victorian shopfront; and for recent examples that attempt to respect the street scene.

Descriptions: to save space, a telegraphic style has been used, omitting 'the', 'a' and often 'house' or 'building'. A 'pair' means a pair of similar or identical houses and points on separate buildings are usually separated by commas or semi-colons; so that, for instance, 'broad window surrounds and oval; keystones and aprons; 10-bay with rusticated doorway' describes three different houses with these features (the last of 10 bays). If the exact date is given for a building, this can usually be seen on the building — under a pediment or over a doorway; and '1693 rainwaterhead' suggests an interesting house, not just interesting ironwork! When the use of a building is mentioned, eg Town Hall, Grammar School, Assembly Room, this is nearly always the use for which the building was built rather than the use it has now — which may even be a shop or garage, and may well change every few years.

The OS maps: reproduced at the original size, six inches to the mile, 1:10,560. Names written W to E, so revealing which few maps are reproduced with N not at the top of the page. The date in the heading is the date the map was published by OS. The maps were made on much smaller sheets than modern OS maps, so there are many towns which fall between two sheets. In addition, the originals from which we worked had been cut and remounted by Victorian librarians on linen backing sheets. We have tried to rejoin them for this book; occasionally this is obtrusive, but better than a 'gutter' through the middle of the map.

The sketch maps: full lines indicate streets worth exploring; arrows show any particular direction to walk streets; asterisks (*) mark buildings asterisked in text. Not to a consistent scale, S shows the starting point (if any).

Architectural terms and details

A member of my evening classes, conscious of my favourite architectural details, ascribed the following stanza to me:

> My heart lifts up at pediments, I'm filled with joy by quoins,
> I'd rather have a Gibbs surround than pockets full of coins;
> But the thing I truly long for amid triumphs and disasters
> Is to see a place consisting of a set of giant pilasters.

So what do these terms mean?

Pediments are the triangular tops derived from the ends of Greek temples and commonly found on classical buildings, frequently topping the porticoes of shire halls, county courts, C18 churches, and almost invariably non-conformist chapels. But they also often mark the centres of terraces and larger town houses, often over a central portion jutting out or in ('advanced' or 'recessed'). I tend to call such town houses 'grand', since pediments were generally used for the great country houses.

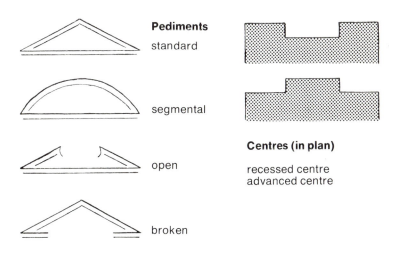

Pediments

standard

segmental

open

broken

Centres (in plan)

recessed centre
advanced centre

Pediments are also used on a smaller scale over windows, sometimes completely detached from the surround, sometimes alternately standard and segmental; and also as a sort of gable end to dormer windows in the roof, again often alternately standard and segmental (particularly in the late C17); and over doorways. Of the four types shown, segmental were a particular feature of Baroque and late C17 houses, and standard and broken are the most common.

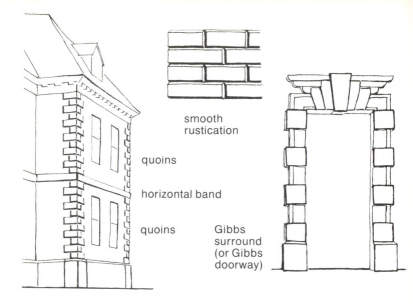

smooth
rustication

quoins

horizontal band

quoins

Gibbs
surround
(or Gibbs
doorway)

Quoins are stones or bricks, often chamfered at an angle, alternately long and short as one goes up the building like medieval flintwork. They mark the corners of the building or of an advanced or recessed centre. They are usually of a different material from the rest of the facade, to give a more varied treatment to the vertical edges. Quoins are occasionally found marking window openings or the sides of a doorway, where they are known, after the architect James Gibbs, as a *Gibbs surround* or Gibbs doorway.

Another surface treatment of a wall is *rustication*, where blocks of stone are left rough or pock-marked as though by bullet holes — to give the impression that they came straight from 'Nature'; or alternatively dressed flush, with horizontal and/or vertical joints — *smooth rustication*, usually on a ground floor to contrast with the floors above.

The vertical structural elements supporting a building are called *piers* (when rectangular in section) and *columns* (when circular in section). Piers and columns, when freestanding, are called *pillars*, whereas *pilasters* are classical 'pillars' incorporated into a wall, as though slapped on, and are usually rectangular in section. They vary from being the almost essential side elements of a Georgian doorway or window, to being used in place of quoins to mark a corner, or an advanced or recessed centre. They may be the full height of the building, in which case they are called *giant pilasters*, which are a particular feature of the Baroque style. If used in pairs, pilasters are said to be coupled.

Usually pilasters and quoins are alternative ways of dealing with corners, but occasionally (a feature of NE Norfolk) they are combined in what one can equally well call *even quoins* (because not alternately long and short) or *rusticated pilasters* (since most pilasters are smooth).

At ground level look out for historic shopfronts, including ornate Victorian ones, and enjoy the rare cases where there are covered walkways, with shops one side and open to the street the other. Usually I give these the Italian term *loggia* (Bologna has 20 miles of them); or if the building on top is supported by columns, then *colonnade*. Occasionally people call them *arcades* but I feel this term is better reserved for completely enclosed pedestrian streets, such as the Burlington Arcade in London.

However the term *arcade* is also used architecturally, for a row of columns or piers linked together with arches, whether the spaces between are open (as in a cathedral arcade) or filled in later, or were designed simply to give interest and relief to a wall—a *blank arcade*. A characteristic feature of historic towns is the free-standing island c17/18 town hall, with first floor council room. This was originally open at ground level for market stalls, and occasionally is still open, but generally the arcade has been filled in. So usually when I mention an arcade, it is 'blank' not 'open'.

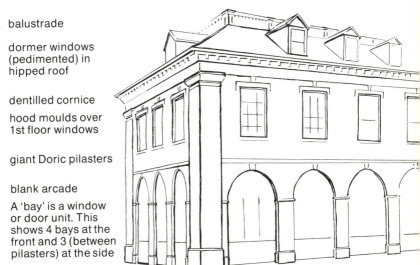

balustrade

dormer windows (pedimented) in hipped roof

dentilled cornice

hood moulds over 1st floor windows

giant Doric pilasters

blank arcade

A 'bay' is a window or door unit. This shows 4 bays at the front and 3 (between pilasters) at the side

In medieval timberframe buildings, look for unusual details such as little wooden buttresses or carved angle posts and horizontal beams (*bressumers*) supporting overhanging floors. In

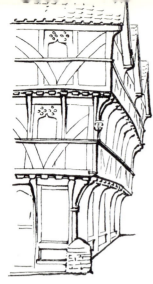

3 gables

bressumer at second overhang
single bracket

bressumer at first overhang

angle post

later houses, look for bow or bay windows, and whether these have little pilasters or a frieze on top. If the house is set back from the street, does it have elaborate iron railings, walls or gatepiers?

The main groundfloor feature is of course the doors and doorways. Some have little flights of steps up to them, with side railings; some of the actual doors are medieval oak with iron hinges or, later, six or eight panels with Gothick details perhaps. The glazing design of the fanlight above the door may be as elaborate as a church window. The most likely part to be original is the door surround, or doorway. If it is medieval stonework, see if the arch has been moulded, whether the infill panels are carved, whether there are heads or foliage in the design. If it is a Georgian doorway, see if the sides are pilasters or pillars, which classical order they are, whether Gibbs, whether the top is pedimented overhanging on carved brackets, with an apsidal or shell hood; whether with a porch jutting forward on columns, sometimes with Regency ironwork—canopies and groundfloor verandahs.

a loggia or
covered walkway:
the columns along
the street form
a colonnade

The classical orders of piers, columns and pilasters were derived from Greek and Roman architecture, and are recognized by their tops or *capitals*. Working from the strongest, simplest and most elemental order towards the more decorative and playful (and architects often moved this way as they progressed up a building) the *Doric* has a simple capital and simple vertical fluting, if any. The *Ionic* is distinguished by its twirly volutes. The *Corinthian* has clustered foliage plus small volutes.

Above the columns or pilasters in a classical temple came a horizontal frieze, the most common being the Doric one of alternating smooth stones and triglyphs, above which was the overhanging cornice. A triglyph frieze may also be found on a porch jutting into the street.

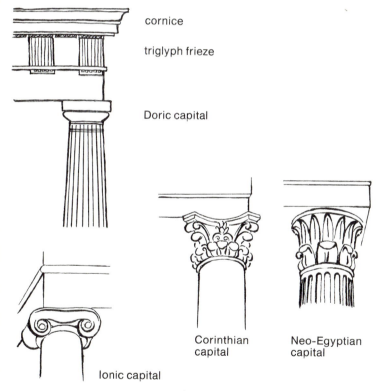

cornice

triglyph frieze

Doric capital

Corinthian capital

Neo-Egyptian capital

Ionic capital

In addition to the three classical orders, there are composite capitals combining all three. In the early c19 a neo-Egyptian capital, like peeling artichokes, was occasionally used, and the architect A H Wilds invented his own 'ammonite' capital with a shell motif, which he used at Brighton, Hove and Lewes.

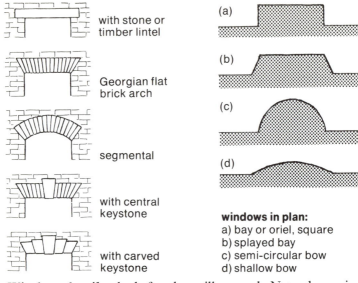

with stone or timber lintel

Georgian flat brick arch

segmental

with central keystone

with carved keystone

(a)

(b)

(c)

(d)

windows in plan:
a) bay or oriel, square
b) splayed bay
c) semi-circular bow
d) shallow bow

Window details: look for those illustrated. Note the various designs for spanning the opening: the segmental top was a late C17/early C18 Baroque feature, replaced by the simpler Georgian flat brick arch, or carved keystones. Then, as a delightful overlap between Georgian and Regency, comes the decorative, usually unmoulded, Gothick style (with a 'k' to distinguish it from the real medieval Gothic and the serious C19 neo-Gothic to come later) which is often combined with exotic 'Moorish' or Chinoiserie. Look for it in shopfronts of the period, or in glazing (for example in the Venetian window illustrated) or in the doubly curved *ogive* windows or door—called *ogee* in C14. In the early Victorian period, windows tended towards greater elaboration again, with surrounds and pedimented tops, especially in the Italianate style favoured by banks.

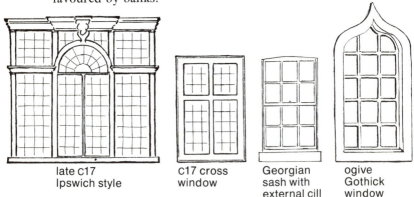

late C17
Ipswich style

C17 cross
window

Georgian
sash with
external cill

ogive
Gothick
window

At the junction of wall and roof, if the roof overhangs the wall, there is often moulded stonework along the top of the wall, immediately under the overhang. If late C17, it often has curved console brackets; if Georgian, often dentilled square-toothed brackets. Alternatively the front wall may continue upwards as a parapet to mask the front gutter, perhaps with panels in relief or lengths of balustrade with urns, or topped by an overhanging cornice. In early C18 Baroque houses, this cornice can be well below the top, to define a low 'attic' storey above. Look out for a different style of windows just below the roof. Whatever the treatment of the top of the front, the roofs must be drained, so look out for rainwaterheads, often giving the date of the building.

The roofs and chimneys, despite the inevitable wires and television aerials, have shapes and silhouettes which are one of the features of historic buildings. Timberframe houses are often jettied out in successive overhangs, or have gables at roof level. The ends of the gable timbers are often masked by decorative *bargeboards*, especially early C19. Look out for chimneystacks in clusters, or with patterned Tudor brickwork, or even occasionally linked together by arches or pilastered.

Scottish medieval or C17 houses often have 'crowstep' gables, and their walls are *harled* (Scottish term for roughcast). The gables are now often painted white. Later Scottish houses, in the Georgian period, tend to be of dressed stone, with straight triangular gables, often divided by the chimney—one could call them pedimented. These Scottish gables frequently face the street, rather than being at right angles to it, giving a distinctively Scottish street scene.

Venetian window, pilastered, with central Gothick glazing

Scottish crowstep gables and carved dormer window

4 South-eastern England

Berkshire

Reading has been spoilt by high growth and redevelopment; but *Hungerford* has a good High Street; and *Newbury* is worth exploring either side of the clocktower on the old Bath Road, s to bridge, w along the canal, E to old river wharf with strange C17 warehouse range, and s round Market Place.

Windsor and Eton (1881): first Eton College area: fine high-density townscape (1) with chapel and narrow street, to fine Georgian houses (2). Then C18 redbrick and C17 gables (3); largely Georgian redbrick group with houses through arches (4)—advanced centre and recess over door, pilasters, neo-Elizabethan front, pedimented stucco. Then becomes small-town high street—good shopfronts, some yellowbrick Georgian: pilasters opposite terrace; Gothick glazing (5), recesses with balcony; 1700s purple/redbrick; C18 almshouses (6); two timberframe (7)—1420s opposite bressumers; good 4½-bay redbrick and columned corner of 'George'.

Across pedestrianised bridge into Windsor. Ironwork and gabled timberframe (8); fine late C17 pedimented house (9). Then large pedimented Georgian (10) opposite stucco with central Egyptian window, pilasters with combined 1st/2nd floor windows; two

Georgian brick with segmental windows and bands. Beyond statue (11) delightful intricate area: in cobbled street 1700s with scroll doorway, 1640s with bay windows on scroll brackets, timberframe and Georgian, opposite good fanlights and bow windows. At end, 'Ship' with recesses; left to 1720s school (12) with niches and curious details; then back past gables and C16 'Three Tuns', to splendid 1680s Town Hall with pilasters not on corners. Opposite, Georgian redbrick with bands, stucco range including pedimented hotel with ironwork (13), curious tall 1st-floor windows, stucco with 'four seasons' relief high up, nice doorways and fanlights, Georgian redbrick behind nasty fascia, stucco with railings (14)—facing C19 stone bank and good new infill.

Then Georgian street to the Park (15): on left, rusticated door surrounds, yellowbrick pub, house with Gothick top; on right, stucco terrace (good corner), pilasters, ironwork, yellowbrick row (good porch), fine doorways, ogive Gothick bay window. Beyond (16) to fine house behind good railings and three terraces: York, yellowbrick, pilastered; Brunswick with 1st-floor canopied verandahs (opposite stucco terrace, villas and hotel); and Adelaide of 1831, facing park, with pilastered and pedimented centre.

Hampshire and the Isle of Wight

Varied materials, with characteristic Georgian redbrick, hung tiles, flintwork. I have not covered *Southampton*, which is a historic city, nor *Portsmouth* with delightful Old Portsmouth. *Fareham* has a fine Georgian High Street and *Gosport* has Regency Alverstoke Crescent. *Petersfield* and *Alresford* are worth exploring, as is *Newport*, Isle of Wight—where *West Cowes* has some Regency houses, and *Ryde* is basically a Regency/early-Victorian resort, with a 28-bay terrace.

Lymington: early C19 redbrick and stucco with bay and bow windows (often 3 bays wide). From The Quay with townscape of yacht masts, up pedestrian Quay Hill to High Street. Uphill towards church cupola: on left, pedimented and pilastered house with ironwork, Venetian window, Victorian bank and shopfront, Georgian with wings, pilasters, nice Church Lane; on right, pair, stucco hotel (ironwork), columned shopfront, iron balcony under canopy, bay window with frieze, fine stucco villa, Georgian redbrick. Facing church, two late C17 houses (quoins, recessed window surrounds; gatepiers and gate; crosswindows); walk to 3 giant stucco arches.

Romsey (1871): an attractive town, with nice plan and much Georgian redbrick. At centre: Gothick shopfront (1), rounded columned corner, pilastered stucco inn (2) and island Corn Exchange. Through flint arch to Venetian window and stucco houses with Gothick glazing (3). S to houses pedimented (4), with garlands everywhere (5). N past Gothick details (6), C13 stone and flint (7) to brewery house (8) and beyond (9). E to two fine houses—with Gibbs windows and aprons (10), yellowbrick with columned porch (11); and past nice cottages (12) to 1540 timberframe (13).

Winchester (1874): cathedral city and superb historic town. Look for bow windows (usually stucco, 1st-floor), Georgian brick window surrounds, early-Victorian curved street corners.

High Street E to W: Alfred statue between almshouses (1), (2); 1871 Guildhall (3), opening (4) to tower, corner columns (5) and frieze. Excellent pedestrian stretch: colonnade (6) opposite pediment; divert to shell porch (7) and good new infill (8). Nice group round Buttercross (9) opposite 7-bay house with pilastered groundfloor (fanlight), medieval timberframe (10); fine shopfront, yellowbrick house with elaborate window (11), 1713 Guildhall with clock on carved bracket. Up to Westgate: double bowfront (12), Georgian houses up lanes (13) and to superb C13 castle hall (14), good stucco (15). Nice loop: pilastered hotel (16), Victorian terrace (17) with ironwork, back past brick rows (18) to obelisk.

Loop N: pitted quoins of 1805 gaol (19) (wing beyond chapel) opposite Venetian window, columned shopfront and pilastered window, Georgian house; 1836 portico (20), Edwardian theatre (21). Past Georgian brewery (22) to C17 gable (23), abbey gateway (24), detached 5-bay house (25). Along North Walls (26), back past terraces (27), Georgian hotel, 1690s shell doorway (28), to corner bay windows (29).

From (2) over bridge to 1744 mill (30); past timberframe (31) to nice green (32). Georgian (33) to stucco house (34) behind C18 gates; fine view from hill (35).

Southgate Street has good Georgian (36), Baroque house (37), early C19 terraces (38). Between this, the High Street, the

cathedral and the College is a delightful largely Georgian redbrick area worth exploring in detail. Then along walls walk (39) past the College, to street (40) and house (41) with giant arch and, in Close, 8 gables (42) facing another 8. Finally Kingsgate Street: timberframe row (43), good shopfronts, 1571 house with stone surrounds (44) to back portico (45); half a mile s to superb C12–15 St Cross Hospital.

Kent

A large county, improving the further one moves from London, with a remote Eastern end and a good set of historic towns. The characteristic materials are stone and flint, timberframe, sometimes exposed but more often faced with timber weatherboarding, or hung with overlapping orange tiles or even mathematical tiles looking like small bricks, which are a Kent-Sussex speciality. Plus the usual Georgian brick, red or often yellow, sometimes with redbrick dressings as in Cambridgeshire.

Good townscape in the high streets of *Hythe*, at *Tonbridge* (N of bridge) and *Sevenoaks* (S of fork). Along the coast are the usual 2 or 3-storey bow windows (usually yellowbrick) and stucco terraces at the seaside resorts: fine 5-storey Waterloo Crescent at *Dover*; and C18 redbrick in Cecil Square (blitzed), 1790s Hawley Square, Fort Hill and Fort Crescent at *Margate*. The best (with first-floor iron verandahs) is at *Ramsgate*: Royal Crescent and Paragon — with behind and inland, delightful Spencer and then Vale Squares; Nelson Crescent with Liverpool Lawn inland; and, N of busy harbour, grand Wellington Crescent with a continuous Doric colonnade; while s at *Pegwell Bay* is an amazing isolated 36-bay Italianate terrace with laurel decorations.

Rochester: many Georgian brick houses with doors and windows in rounded recesses. Start with bridge chapel and Grecian stucco house facing river, then into High Street. Fine 1687 Guildhall with segmental pediment and open ground floor opposite Georgian inn; unusual Venetian window of 'George'; house with stucco ribbon and wreaths (*); delightful 1706 Corn Exchange with cupola and clock over street. Beyond cathedral gate: nice bow shopfront; redbrick with pilasters and aprons; almshouse courtyard (*); to town walls both sides. Then spectacular overhanging timberframe both sides — one side part of fine museum complex (*); to fine stucco house with tripartite windows, steps and wings (*). Up Star Hill: Georgian yellowbrick houses (and along New Road into Chatham). Back and uphill to

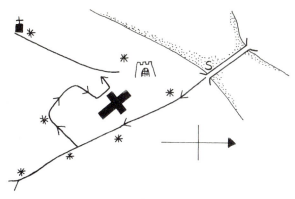

house with elaborate gabled c17 facade (*), next to shell porch; through garden (town wall behind) into cathedral close to Georgian terrace. Through medieval gateway up street with good houses to rendered Georgian house (*)—classical pedimented one side, Gothick battlemented the other (from park behind church). Back down to good houses (*) facing Norman castle keep.

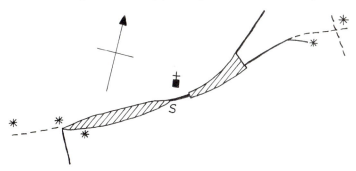

Tenterden: an attractive little town with long tree-lined High Street—timberframe and Georgian, brick and stucco, weatherboarded, tilehung or faced with mathematical tiles. Start at narrowing, where 2-storey bow window is opposite timberframe with oriel. NE: Town Hall loggia opposite mathematical tiles with hoist and wooden quoins, bowfront, good porch; left fork good (9-bay terrace) out to Venetian window and chapel; right fork to 1848 terrace and good individual houses (*)—redtile with Venetian and whirling round windows, rusticated wooden facade. SW of church: overhanging row, cottages behind gardens opposite white houses with bow and bay windows; groundfloor recesses (*), near pedimented windows over doors; two fine individual houses (*)—1700s with twirly windowtop, pilastered 1711 with elaborate centre; nice to the left, out to castellated bow window (at back).

Canterbury (1877): many fine timberframe and Georgian houses within walls (and just outside) but also much bad redevelopment and many open carparks.

Walk A Follow walls: on top (1), round from outside (2), behind houses (3); along line past timberframe Wealden house (4), with houses built into towers (5), superb Westgate (6); round (7) to castle keep (8).

Walk B from cathedral close gate (9) and little cobbled square. First down delightful overhanging lane to pargetted timberframe

(10) and good group opposite house with neo-Egyptian windows (11). Up street to group with stucco pilasters (12). To medieval hospital (13) (behind, Greyfriars over river), lane with coat of arms (14), 1708 almshouses with Dutch gables (15), attractive churchyard (16) to (8). Houses built into wall (Gothick glazing, Dutch gable), nice group near pub (17), Regency stucco houses (18) in gardens—pilasters, one Gothick with battlements. To terrace with giant arches (19) in good street, becoming largely timberframe (20). To c17 house with Doric entablature (21); good frontage (22) and street.

Walk C Start at (9). Good mixed (23), redevelopment, to Georgian redbrick and carved timberframe (24); nice streets to monastery gateways (25) (26), timberframe Wealden house (27). Across roundabout, beside 1574 timberframe (28) into attractive area (29), to Gothick house (30), back past redbrick row (31).

Walk D Start at (9); chapel with Egyptian windows (32); largely timberframe frontage—one with beasties (33)—to fine corner (34), good mixed (35), off to nice street (3), out to hospital with courtyard (36). From (34) down redbrick street with new infill, to Blackfriars (37).

Walk E From superb Norman hospital on bridge (38): timberframe over river and up lane (39); 1811 chapel (40); figure brackets both sides (41); to 3-storey bow window (42) and giant Ionic columns (43). Beyond Westgate nice mixed frontage (44); Georgian loop along river (45) back to 'Falstaff' (46). Fine timberframe (47); to medieval brick gateway next to giant arches (48). Into delightful Regency area—to Gothick house (49), past terrace (50) with iron balconies to good Georgian frontage (51).

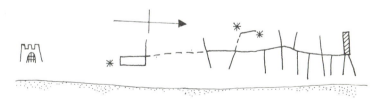

Deal: an extraordinary late c17 grid seatown, with attractive 2-storey c18 houses. Walk along seafront, with boats on shingle beach, and, as shown on map, along Middle Street, looking both sides: block N of signal tower (*); then past gaps to N of Market Street through even texture at least to The Square. Inland at Oak Street (nasty gap) to High Street stretch with 1803 Town Hall on loggia (*) and Georgian house with two 3-storey bay windows, pedimented at top (*).

Tunbridge Wells (1872): a c17 spa, with attractive common and delightful Regency/early Victorian residential areas near town centre. Start at pedestrian Pantiles (1)—flagstones and brick setts, weatherboarding, hung tiles, good shopfronts plus good stucco frontage (2) with hotel (pilasters, ironwork, porches). Then above church: 3 fine villas (3)—Gothick porches, shell pilastered, pebbledash; good stucco (4); little redbrick terrace (5) with bow windows; good 1830s villas (6) up to earlier Georgian house (7) and The Grove (8). Down, then up 1870s road (9) to fine Tuscan church portico (10). Back to Decimus Burton's 1829 Holy Trinity (11), next to Gothick villa—beginning of his impressive Calverley scheme (all in stone): 6-bay house (12) opposite hotel with columned porch; 30-bay crescent (13) with advanced centre and 'promenade'; down to his disfigured Town Hall scheme (14)—7-bay flanked by two villas each side, all pedimented. Finally through arch (15) to the climax—the marvellous *rus in urbe* of the curve of 19 villas (16) facing rough parkland plus rhododendrons (compare with municipal park below), all inventively different in their plans and combinations of bow and bay windows, canopies and verandahs.

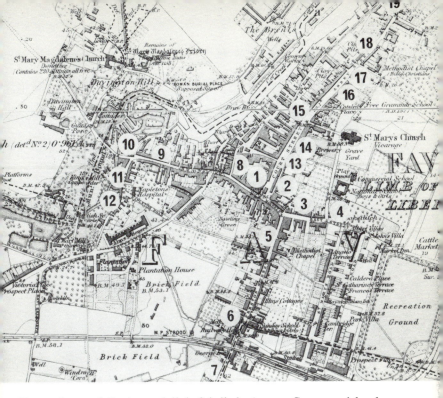

Faversham (1877): a delightful little town. Start at island Guildhall on timber columns; through medieval stone door, timberframe courtyard (1); in Middle Row, house with huge keystones (2). First E to red/yellowbrick with pilasters (3) and grand house with Venetian windows in wings (4). Then commercialised Preston Street: several timberframe (5), out to fine Georgian redbrick houses with columned porches, with round and bow windows (6), two more beyond railway underpass (7). Then pedestrian largely timberframe West Street: 1697 pargetting (1); exposed timberframe down lane (8); curious balustrade dormer window (9); nice redbrick warehouses (10), little terraces (11), overhanging timberframe row (12). Finally, and best, to N. Good group with pedimented doorway (13); brewery house with fluted tripartite windows (14) into famous well cared-for Abbey Street, with cobbles and trees. Two-storey tall bay windows (15); three shallow tripartite bow windows (16) plus 1598 door with beasties; stone and timberframe Arden's house (17); nice 1850 brick rows (18); to C18 warehouse on quay (19).

Sandwich (1877): a delightful intricate walled medieval town—largely 2-storey stucco or brick painted white. Walk along line of walls (tree-lined, with moat) and explore in great detail excellent streets (1–4) and E of that line, plus The Strand out to 1580s gabled school (5). Note: carved brackets on 'Kings Arms' (4); marvellous timber frame group (6); bridge barbican (7); water gate (8) plus cobbled street; elaborately patterned C17 Dutch House (9); and Gothick flint house (10).

Surrey

The few historic towns there were are now largely wrecked by London commuter growth. *Guildford* has its superb High Street—its 1683 Guildhall with cupola and overhanging clock, Tuscan portico opposite, up to 1620s gatehouse. *Godalming* is delightful round island Market Hall, N to church, E into first part of High Street; and *Dorking* is worth exploring in all directions from W end of High Street—both towns having some C17 houses with crude pilasters.

Farnham (1873): basically Georgian, largely redbrick, plus much neo-Georgian, such as Town Hall (1) with loggia; nearby recreated C17 with Dutch gable, niches, pilasters opposite grand yellowbrick 'Bush' (2). Up delightful street to medieval castle/palace: stucco, wide brick arches (3); good redbrick (4) becoming Victorian stucco (5) to pediment (6). Returning: two good houses (7) with stone scroll doorway, ogive bay window (Gothick glazing) and balustrade; nice lane (8); gabled almshouses and Georgian recessed arches (9); tilehung timberframe, good shopfronts near (1). Then timberframe gables (10) opposite Venetian and bow windows with friezes.

Into fine West Street: timberframe inn with courtyard (11); tall arches masking early C19 shopfront (12) and stucco next to nice lane; round window and frieze, Venetian window (13). Returning: recesses with roundel frieze (14) and two finest houses (15): pedimented centre, windows and doorway; segmental surrounds, rusticated pilasters. Then stucco pair, C18 library and railings (16); pair with band and frieze; recessed centre; lunettes and Venetian window next to good shopfront, aprons (17), stucco with recesses. S to little redbrick terraces, cobbles, past church (18) out to segmental double fanlight (19) and good group (20)—3-storey redbrick (1717) with elaborate centre, C19 yellowbrick with splayed quoined doorway. Over bridge to converted maltings (21) and Cobbett's birthplace (22) with Gothick glazing, timber gable, round arches.

Sussex

A long county, administratively two. The local materials are timberframe (both exposed and plastered), hung tiles, some flint, some weatherboarding particularly in East Sussex and, surprisingly, some stone, including Horsham 'slates', found there in the famous Causeway. Unlike Surrey, its position within commuting distance of London has caused its towns to be well cared for, rather than wrecked.

The Regency developments of Brighton and Hove are too extensive to be covered as explained on page 13.

Hastings has delightful Old Town (fine High Street), the strange timber net stores on the beach, 1824 Pelham Crescent followed by Decimus Burton's classical stucco hotels and the villas of St Leonards. *Worthing* has fine Park Crescent and Liverpool Terrace of the same date. Of the smaller towns (not mentioned below) the best are *Battle* (in and around Market Place); and *Steyning* with a good long High Street plus excellent street to grand Norman church.

Chichester (1880): Georgian (and neo-Georgian) — usually redbrick, some stucco and flint. Four Roman streets meet at 1501 Market Cross. Almost complete walls, with Inner Ring Road round them; walk Northern half, visiting C13 Greyfriars choir (1) and castle motte (2).

Four main streets (W and N being the best). East St: 2-storey bay window over columns plus shopfront (3); twirly windowtops, bow windows (4); portico (5); stucco pair, blue/redbrick with pilasters (6); to irregular St Pancras area. South St: timberframe

overhanging row (7), chequerbrick and stucco pairs (8) opposite 2-storey recessed centre on columns, flint with bow window, theatre pediment. West St: stucco 'Dolphin' (9)—8-bay centre; excellent doorways plus Venetian window (10), segmental recesses (11); 1696 mansion (12) with crosswindows, volutes; beyond IRR, good as far as large house with 1751 centre (13). North St: colonnaded Market House (14) and Council House (15); twirly windowtops (16); good stretch (17) with bow and bay windows—several (one Gothick) over good doorways; big flint and yellowbrick (18); stucco with recessed porch (19); two 3-storey bay windows (20). Off map: C17 almshouses, sculptural modern theatre.

Within the quadrants: NW: C20 county buildings. SW: cathedral precinct. The last two quadrants have excellent Georgian brick. NE: from (15) to little square (21) near extraordinary medieval hospital (22); past pilasters (23); (24) to pedimented (25); (26), (27). SE: past rusticated recesses (28), into Pallants and grand 1712 house (29). Past cottages to big house (30) in grounds. Varied columned porches (31) opposite pediment. Past twirly window-tops, twin-columned doorway (32) to little terrace (33), to good houses (34).

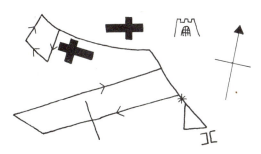

Arundel: superb from distance, capped by castle, parish church, C19 RC cathedral. Much C19 redbrick/timberframe, but also good houses of Georgian brick and stucco, flint, some weatherboarded and timberframe. Fine townscape (good shopfronts) uphill from cross (*): redbrick ('Norfolk Arms' lettering, pair, Venetian windows) opposite mixed (yellowbrick with balustrade). First up stone castlewall to C19 Gothick and RC cathedral, loop left into nice flint cottage area. Then loop from (*) to main streets: Tarrant, to good stretch; little 1821 stone terrace. Back by Maltravers with raised pavements: stucco pilastered row; good redbrick opposite one with wings (shell Venetian window); pilastered terrace; bay (some weatherboarded) and bow windows; gaol-like neo-Norman council offices.

Lewes (1878): many timberframe houses hung with mathematical tiles, as in Kent. Basically one excellent street along ridge. From church (1) trees, Gothick bowfront opposite stucco pilasters (2); 1577 porch and flint Georgian (3); C15 timberframe (4); neo-Egyptian columns (5) opposite 'Bull' with carved figures; bow and bay windows; 5-bay with lunette (6); shell pilaster tops (7) and pair with mathematical tiles; through C14 barbican to castle (8). Then tilehanging (9); C18 Pelham house (10); stone pedimented (11) and 1800s County Hall (recessed columned entrance, figures)—its parapet higher in centre, as on inn opposite; Venetian window, 1790s tower (12). Beyond cross segmental doorway plus bow windows, big surrounds opposite two grand 5-bay (13) one with twirly windowtops; stucco recesses and terrace (14) with ironwork. Fine Georgian houses (15)—stone surrounds, Venetian window, strange hybrid pair (16).

Over bridge to nice street (17)—varied pilasters, colonnade; to redbrick chapel (18), slatehung uphill (19), rusticated stucco (20). Then back to (4) and down steep cobbled street (21)—almshouses to spectacular C16 stone Grange (22). 20-bay pilastered crescent (23) to attractive street: honeysuckle frieze and capitals (24), brick recesses; good exposed timberframe (25). Off ridge nice mid C19 brick terrace areas (26).

Rye (1878): a superb hilltown with marvellous textures — weatherboarding and timberframe, brick, tiles, plaster, cobbled streets, and views out over the surrounding main roads, round line of walls. Explore within in great detail. Two good approaches up to large cruciform church. First from little redbrick crescent and stucco row N of railway bridge (1); weatherboarding and stucco; through C14 Landgate (2); view to boats, good brick (3) — pair, yellowbrick bank; C18 bow shopfront (4); C15 inn (5), 1743 Town Hall on arcade; C15 Fletcher's house (6) and clock quarter-boys.

Second approach from delightful timber, brick, stone warehouses (7); up famous Mermaid Street (8) — fine timberframe 'Mermaid' with courtyard; past Henry James' house (9) — pilasters, urns, aprons. Round churchyard: fine timberframe; Georgian brick cistern oval and dome; C13 Ypres tower (10). Down good street (11) with 1817 redbrick chapel, to town walls (7). Finally the spine (tarmac!): exposed timberframe plus 3 plastered gables (12); cobbled lane up to 'Mermaid', Gibbs round windows and door; fine street (13); yellowbrick and bow windows of 'George'; C17 school with pilasters and Dutch gables (14) opposite fine street; back to (4), down to stone friary (15).

East Grinstead: basically modern, but with good Old Town: excellent historic High Street near church — good exposed timberframe, weatherboarding, raised pavement, trees. Explore E from C17 stone and C16 timber gables (on corner of West Street): round tilehung island, to Georgian 'Dorset Arms', best timberframe group (two overhangs) and stone house; good group in lane with 1619 college (fine courtyard).

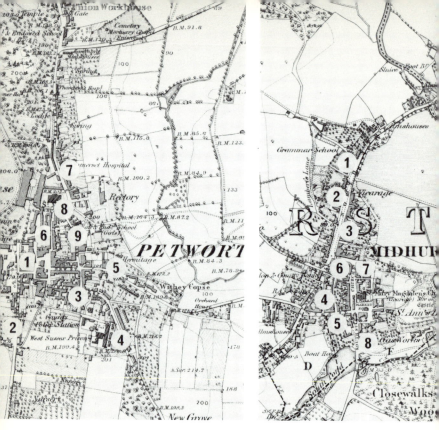

Midhurst (1879): makes a delightful pair with Petworth—
purple/redbrick, tilehanging, timberframe, some stone, with
intricate plans. Battlemented stone with C17 brick gable (1),
Georgian redbrick (2) with Venetian windows, good shopfronts
(3). Then *either* by timberframe lane (4), and Gothick windows
and timberframe dated 1666 (5), *or* past blank arches (6) and
library (7), arriving at marvellous area with islands round the
church: old and new market halls; big surrounds and overhanging
timberframe of 'Spread Eagle'; 7-bay redbrick with stone
pilasters. Good group (8) near pool.

Petworth (1880): sally out from Market Place (1); Town Hall
with round arches, good frontage with wisteria, pediments. To
contrasting fine Georgian stone and redbrick (2). Past tilehung
corner (3) to stone cottage rows (4) (further out, on right,
spectacular C18 New Grove). Out to RC church (5). Finally good
loop: cobbled and tilehung (6) to churchtower; round to fine C17
redbrick almshouses and gabled stone house dated 1653 (7); back
past art-nouveau lamp standard (8) to fine Georgian redbrick (9).

5 Southern and South-western England

Cornwall

Apart from its famous coastline, it is a county of small towns, almost all worth exploring, with two distinctive local materials—slates (often hung on buildings), and granite, used simply (because it is difficult to carve) and effectively in most of its public buildings. *Lostwithiel* has good North and Fore streets with c18 guildhall; *Liskeard* nice houses round central square and *Bodmin* a pleasant area between the church and Assize Court square. *Penryn* has an excellent long Georgian street, from the Square uphill past the island Town Hall to the Terrace; and *Helston* an attractive wide main street with running water both sides—from the park up to the Town Hall, whence a good street to the church. In *Fowey* explore the intricate area between the church and sea, and along Fore Street to the custom house; several medieval houses.

Truro (1888): Pearson's fine late Victorian cathedral with its three French and Gothic spires was sited to include an aisle of the parish church (1), so there is no precinct and it dominates the attractive central area. Fine Georgian Assembly Rooms at its w end; to sw, pilastered Museum (2) and delightful Regency Walsingham Place (3). E of commercial Boscawen Street two fine pedimented houses (4, 5); and beyond the river some nice terraces (6). But best is Georgian granite Lemon Street (7) uphill to Doric column and Regency stucco terrace (8).

Penzance (1890): largely Regency white stucco, its main commercial Market Jew Street builds up well from the station (1) up to the superb 1836 island Market House (2) with portico and dome. From here explore: uphill to Regency houses (3) with Doric doorways, and down Clarence Street; to North Parade and gardens (4); and SE to Market Hall (5), the extraordinary Egyptian house (6), down fine Chapel Street to the church (7), an attractive area below it, and along the coast to Regent Terrace (8) with a square unexpectedly behind (doors with slim cast-iron columns).

St Ives: the classic fishing town, favoured by hippies and painters. It has an intricate and dense street pattern with superb textures: granite, cobbles, tunnels and alleys, slate-hung walls, white cottages; nice names — Virgin and Teetotal Streets.

Falmouth: a good single street along the harbour — from the Moor (centre) past the King Charles church to the fine C18 brick Grove Place and ruined manor house: some excellent white Doric, including the Custom House, early C19 as is Bar Terrace nearer the docks, and some small terraces inland uphill.

Launceston: a Norman hilltop castle town and the county town until 1835. Intricate and attractive streets down to the lavish church; S to a stretch of town wall with gate; NW to spectacular Georgian houses (one with Venetian doorway and eagle gateposts), out to bridge and original settlement of St Stephen.

Devon

A huge varied county, with surprisingly little stone (for SW), but rather stucco, brick and cob (mixed clay and straw), usually painted. *Plymouth* has now only the delightful Barbican area. *Torquay* has a Regency terrace, as has *Teignmouth*. Of the smaller towns *Bideford* has some early C19 stucco S of its long medieval bridge; and an attractive loop N—along quay, past 1690s houses of Bridgeland Street, to return by Mill and High Streets; *Axminster* has an irregular plan and hill site plus two grand C18 houses with Venetian windows.

Barnstaple (1889/90): an attractive area within line of its walls (1). From the Square (2): to 1708 Queen Anne's Walk with colonnade (3); and two good streets to former Northgate: High Street (4) with pedimented 1820s Guildhall and C17/18 houses above shopfronts; and curving Boutport Street (1) with C18 houses, medieval stone vicarage, early C19 hotels. Between, church with C17 almshouses (5), and mid-C19 Butcher's Row colonnade (6) and market hall. From the Square SE: stucco terrace facing river (7); behind, intimate street with splendid C17 almshouses (8) on loggia; further out to more Regency terraces (9) and linked classical villas facing green square.

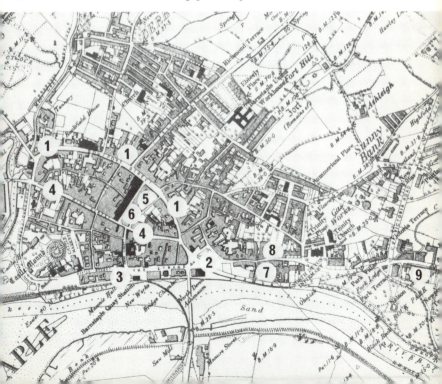

Exeter (1890): like Gloucester, it has been so strenuously and badly redeveloped that its most attractive area is now the canal; but there is much to explore, including the almost complete line of walls and some good Georgian—with a characteristic round Gibbs doorway with heads and groundfloor recessed arches. From medieval bridge (1) past good timberframe (2) to more timberframe, pilasters in Fore Street and an elaborate Georgian facade (3) high up. Left past Priory (4) to churchyard lined by Georgian brick and stucco (5); along walls (6), across iron bridge (7) past good group (8) to stucco villa with loggia (9); back through pleasant Victorian area to terrace (10) and neo-classical stone and neo-Gothic brick (11).

Then through gardens (12) outside walls and castle, past nice houses (13) near castle gateway (fine C18 Assize Courts), to gardens in castle moat (14), across through Doric portico (15) and good new shopping centre to High Street: exuberant C19 and good C17 timberframe, C17 Guildhall (16) overhanging pavement, redbrick house (17) with segmental pediment, quoins, aprons. Down overhanging alley to fine houses round cathedral (18, 19), and delightful Georgian area: gardens, terraces—characteristic brick (20), stucco with loggia (21), crescent (22), fine hospital facade (23). Finally to almshouses with courtyard (24), only bit of old South Street (25), across traffic and off map (26) to terrace above river, down to quay (C17 custom house, C18 warehouses), across ferry to canal and maritime museum.

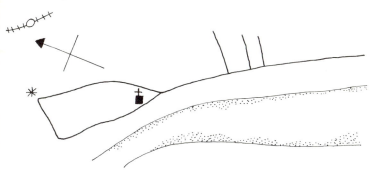

Topsham: five miles S and technically part of Exeter. A delightful C17–18 port. Explore streets shown. From fine Georgian houses (railings *): street SW past little stucco square to good houses near shore. Fine Fore Street to S: mixed timberframe, Georgian redbrick and stucco; Venetian window over inn entrance; blank arches; at bend good inn porch opposite tall redbrick houses. Then the Strand—shell door, bay and bow windows, rusticated pilasters, hung slates and characteristic shaped gables, to good stucco villas at end.

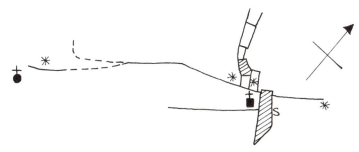

Tavistock: a delightful town of stucco and grey-green stone. Good square with abbey gatehouse, C19 town hall, castellated library and hotel. SW past Gothick villas to attractive canal head. NE past Victorian terrace and row between two stucco houses with quoins to good curved corner shopfront (*). Beyond church, nice main street to SW: pilastered corner (*) and 1835 Cornmarket (*) with nice area (good shopfronts) up behind both; attractive (pilasters) out to 1762 almshouses (*), near RC church.

Totnes (1888): a delightful little town with a clear line of walls (1) with two gates (10 and 13); like Dartmouth, timberframe and painted C17–18 often slatehung. From bridge (2), first E to timberframe between stone buttresses (3), pilastered terrace (4) and good stucco (5). W of bridge an attractive square: stucco— bows, pilasters; stone warehouses and C18 segmental windows (6). Then superb townscape sequence up main street, from an elaborate inn porch with room over (7); pilasters, bow and bay windows, Gothick house up lane (8); Georgian redbrick with Venetian window (9) opposite one with huge coffered porch behind pineapples; best timberframe and Gothick gateway (10); crude 1707 pilasters and keystone heads (11). Behind church, C17 Guildhall (1) on columns, above walls. Then delightful slatehung loggias over pavements (12). To N, town gate (13) and castle (14). Then pilasters, timberframe, tilehanging (Venetian window) round corner (15) to stucco terrace (16) and 2 good villas.

Sidmouth: a Regency seaside resort—stucco, ironwork (veran-dahs), bow windows, Gothick details and many fine villas outside centre. Start along the Esplanade from E: redbrick terrace (like Weymouth) with loggia; delightful Gothick Beach House (*); 3-storey bows. Follow green inland: ogive canopies; a terrace linked by columns to pedimented villas; two fine redbrick houses next to gardens (*), near 3 battlemented villas (Gothick doorshafts) facing little pedimented terrace. Past church into town centre—pilasters, bows, to wide High Street and pedimented C18 house with unusual bay/entrance (*).

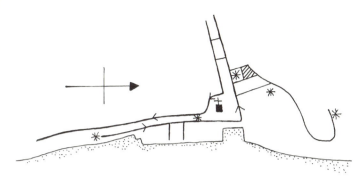

Dartmouth: much timberframe, painted C17–18 (often slate-hung), and early C19 terraces. Explore all streets shown on map. Start at the boat harbour and the Quay (brick pilasters; battlemented hotel with bow windows over columns). Inland: Buttermarket, carved beasts on granite loggia; delightful round and in pannier market (*) with cobbled square and stone arcades; early C19 terraces (as also overlooking sea). To N nice Foss Street (pediment; at end *redbrick* house* with bay window), round and up to 1866 house incorporating earlier timbers (*). To s attractive round church (pediment), Higher Street with many fine overhanging timberframe (best with oriels on brackets *), and along, overlooking sea, past neo-Tudor school to 4 bow windows. Down steps to Bayard's Cove and fort (*), cobbles, good group with pedimented Custom House. Return by Lower Street (to right Venetian doorway; shell door)—pilasters and more timberframe, to a house with 1st-floor wooden columns.

Dorset

An attractive county with a marvellous set of unspoilt country market towns, and *Poole*, which has a good Georgian 'Old Town' harbour area, with good new infill trying to repair the ravages of 1950s and 1960s.

Bridport: many Georgian houses, some stone, some redbrick. From nice sharp edge marked by buildings next to stream, broad East Street (A35) climbs up to fine Town Hall with niches and cupola: s side, brick mansion with stone dressings, bank with neo-Egyptian pilasters; N side, stone Institute with door merged into rustication, unspoilt C18 shopfront. Then broad commercial West Street (Venetian windows s side) down to narrowing by stone ropery N side. From Town Hall follow South Street past Regency chapel and houses and fine C16 stone Museum, to Quaker chapel opposite the church, beyond which is curious stone chantry (setback).

Weymouth (1868): three parts to explore. First the original, medieval port s of the bridge. To w, old High Street (1) blitzed by new Municipal Offices, but, beyond, C17 inn, tiny old Town Hall, good houses. E along harbour, many small bowfronted houses (2), and inland two fine C17 stone houses (3). Secondly, over bridge (4), to Melcombe Regis, the core and shopping centre of present town, worth exploring in detail between George III statue (5), seafront, St Thomas Street, and w to C17/19 'White Hart' (6); bowfronts along seafront (7) and on tip (8); warehouses (9), old fish market and custom house along quay, fine Guildhall (10) and 'Golden Lion' behind. Good street (11): church (cupola), bow windows above shopfronts, C19 classical bank, stucco pilasters on corner.

Finally spectacular seafront, from (5) to (12), of first English seaside resort, with characteristic two-storey bow windows — in brick (unlike Brighton's stucco and Scarborough's stone): 17×3 bays; hotel with Venetian windows; 17×3 with good ironwork broken by huge 1890s hotel; 15×3; 1820s 16×3. Finally, off map, grander, later stone Victoria Terrace.

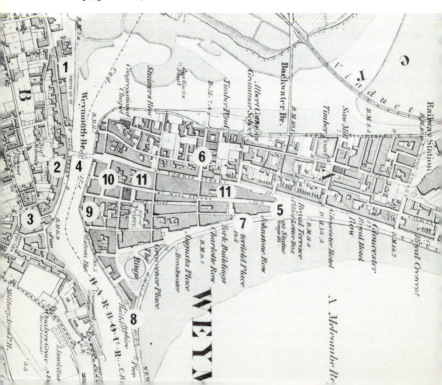

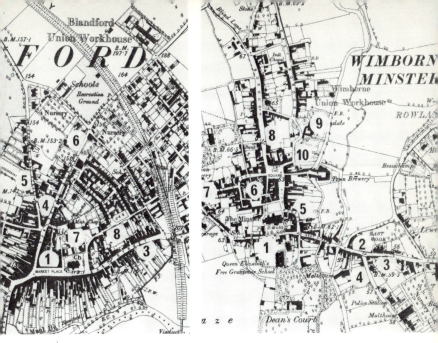

Wimborne Minster (1887): an attractive intricate street pattern round The Square and the massive Minster, with good brick and stucco houses. S of churchyard brick and timber gables (1), and to fork (2): on to thatched turnpike cottage and classical porch (3); to good fanlight by nice sharp edge of town (4). High Street (5) curves nicely with medieval C17/C18 museum. To Cornmarket with C18 Market Hall (6), West Street (7), back past 'Kings Head' to The Square. Finally good loop: up fine Georgian West Borough past house with recessed arches (8); to 1830s house (9) near new bridge; back down curving East Borough past magnificent columned porch (10).

Blandford Forum (1887): rebuilt after 1731 fire by the Bastard brothers, two local Baroque architect/surveyors. Market Place (1): N side has stone Town Hall flanked by characteristic post-fire brick houses; S side has 3 elaborate pilastered houses (Rococo stucco, two brick) opposite fine church. Four sallies recommended. Past neo-Georgian 'Crown' (2) to bridge. Secondly, beyond church to house with curved parapet set back (3). Thirdly up to fork (4); whence left to 1730s blue/redbrick (5) opposite Venetian windows; right past C17 almshouses to two fine houses on left (6). Finally N of churchyard: two good houses opposite Coupar house (7) with red and purple brick and stone dressings behind piers with urns; and to C17 moulded brick Old House (8) with Georgian house beyond.

Dorchester (1888): fine High Street with every material and style
represented. Best from the river at the bottom (1), to the Victorian
stone climax of the churches, Town Hall and Museum (2); then a
fine timberframe group, becoming plain Georgian past Shire Hall
(and 1880s Agriculture House) to roundabout (3). From (2)
attractive South Street with two-storey 'Antelope' bow windows
and 1900s banks opposite fine Georgian fronts and converted
almshouses; good Georgian houses in parallel street (4) and E (5).
Finally the splendid tree-lined walks along the line of the Roman
walls—from County Hall (6) at NW (see complex Colliton house),
past (3) to early C19 stucco villas (7), fine house (8), to corner (9);
back to (1) and/or to nice green by fine Fordington church (10).

Sherborne (1887): delightful, stone-built—its medieval and
Victorian Gothic buildings giving it the character of a medieval
abbey town. From medieval conduit/market cross (1) explore:
past remarkable 1520s tenements to almshouses (2); to 1830s
house (3). Best up Cheap Street: white bowfront with Venetian
window, timberframe/stone medieval house on corner (4), past
elaborate Georgian front to tithe barn (5). Back and to 1800s
bowfronts and C16 library with strange bay window (6). Round
island and W: C17 gabled house (7), nice terrace (8) down to
attractive cottages and raised pavements (9).

E of Cheap Street, less urban but many good houses: Newland past grandest C18 house (10), medieval oriel window to C18 houses (11) facing garden; and Long Street past Tudor house, brewery, redbrick house with stone dressings (12), to redbrick hotel (13). Continues past pleasant cottages to good group (14) by church near castle.

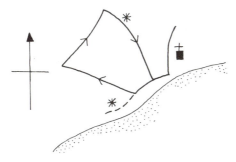

Lyme Regis: an attractive 'watering place' *beside* rather than *facing* the sea. Only one Regency house on front (*); nice warehouse and jetty sw at the Cobb. So it is best to start at church, down past Tudor hotel, tiny guildhall/museum to bridge (and sea). Then island with overhanging house and up the main road, Broad Street, with several blue stone buildings, bow-fronted 'Three Cups', and bay window of 'Royal Lion'. From fork at top of Broad Street, attractive loop inland back past good classical chapel (*).

Shaftesbury (1886): on a hill with only its centre urban (1), by Town Hall and church with timberframe house, grand stucco 'Grosvenor' on loggia (2), High Street (3) with a Georgian stone facade (shallow bow window); behind it, attractive stone cottages (4). But the abbey (5) is an empty ruin, and the best walk is w into the country: past fine Georgian and C17 houses (6) to long 1500s range (7); downhill to a medieval suburb (8), with good houses and nice quadrangle round pump; to ascend Gold Hill (9), with marvellous textures—cobbles, buttresses of abbey wall.

Wareham (1888): a small brick town with lots of space within its Saxon earth ramparts. Walk round defences, and then explore from centre (1): past C16 rubble and brick houses to St Martin's (2), and down through gap to bridge; down good Georgian street to defences (3)—notice whitebrick with redbrick dressings 'Red Lion' with the reverse opposite. Best past C18 stone with elaborate door (4) opposite bowfronted inn, to little square (5) and the Quay (6).

Gloucestershire

Gloucester, which was largely wrecked by bad redevelopment, and *Cheltenham*, with its extensive Regency developments, are not covered—see pages 13–14. At the other extreme the county is famous—too famous in the summer—for its delightful Cotswold stone urban villages. Some consist basically of superb main streets: *Chipping Campden* with market hall and islands and good almshouses towards church, *Winchcombe, Northleach, Moreton-in-Marsh, Broadway* (Worcestershire), *Burford* (Oxfordshire) with good streets either side as well, and less known (and now in Avon) *Chipping Sodbury* (explore from narrowing at top of hill down to T junction, whence left round dogleg to Tudor house, right to bend); and further E, *Corsham* (Wiltshire)—explore to church and left beyond pedestrian area to S, to strange almshouses/school. Others of these villages have a more complex plan and are best explored equally in many directions, including round their churchyards: from their central market places at *Stow-on-the-Wold, Lechlade* and *Fairford*, and E of main road at *Painswick*.

Cirencester: overwhelming in the number and quality of its Cotswold stone buildings—C17 with gables and crosswindows, and Georgian with fine doorways, many grand with pediments; but also some stucco and timberframe. Start in Market Place—N side pilasters, S first-floor Gibbs windows, Venetian window,

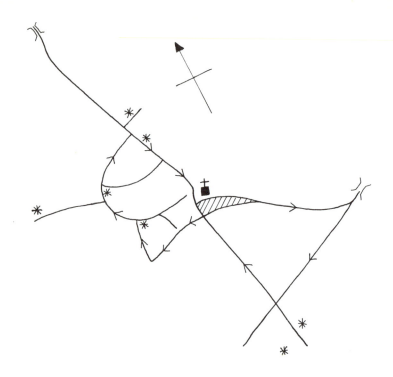

heads and masks on keystones, and the incredible church (inside as wide and high as it is long). Two sallies recommended, second better.

SE and S. Past timberframe 'Bear' to good group opposite new shops, later good houses to bridge; nice terraces and rows in Lewis Lane; left to almshouses (*), on to good group with warehouses; back commercialised but on left early C18 7-bay house with curious surrounds, pedimented door.

Second N and W. W to park wall past good group with 8 gables and C17 school, to Gothick windows on corner (*). Double back past grand Georgian house (fine Roman museum) to church tower, right to fork seen earlier. Along park wall past fine houses (ovals) to spacious Cecily Hill: 1802 Tontine terrace, 1857 battlemented barracks (*). Past interesting corner (*), up and down superb curving C17 Coxwell Street. Continuing past two grand pedimented Georgian, left along fine street—increasingly small-scale cottages—out to bridge. Returning, left to C12 arcade (*), past house with elliptical segmental window and doortops (*), back to church tower.

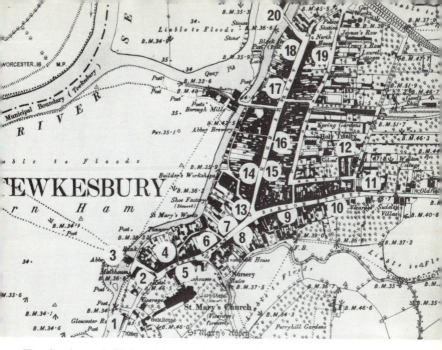

Tewkesbury (1884): with superb abbey church, but outstanding also for many overhanging exposed timberframe houses (several carved door spandrels), typically having flattish roofs and huge oriel windows on one or more floors, plus Georgian (fine coaching inns), redbrick (carved keystones, Venetian and tripartite windows) and stucco. And, confined to w and s by the flood plain, for its remarkable courts and alleys along the narrow burgage plots. Explore at least the following alleys during your walk: Old Baptist Chapel (4); Ancil's and Lilley's (8); Compton's, Fletcher's, Hughes, Fish, Yarnell's (9); Walls (15); Clark's (17) plus Red Lane; Stephen's to Gothick cottage (19).

From redbrick group (1), 'Bell' (2) and lane to weatherboarded mill (3); remarkable pre-1539 range (5)—two Georgian infill, and little crescent; fine early c18 (6), c15 with timber tracery, inn porch (7). Then Georgian front with timberframe yard (first-floor balustrade), double bow shopfront (9), museum with wooden railings, another bowfront (10) to stucco rows (11) and 1830s knitting 'topshops' (12). Back to fine corner timberframe (13), clock and strange Georgian windows; tall gabled timberframe, 'Swan' (14), stone Town Hall with bell and urns; neo–Tudor front (15), vista to recessed church front (16). Opposite new shops, hotel (17) with 1701 facade (cross windows, broken pediment), double bowfront, two fine doorways/fanlights (18). Past timberframe corner to medieval bridge (20).

Tetbury (1886): a delightful little stone-built Cotswold town with an intricate plan and the same mixture of buildings as Cirencester. First good loop—from island Market House on squat pillars, opposite two tall 3-storey C17 gables (1). N into The Chipping—good houses including little rendered terrace (2) and fine Georgian (3); down cobbled lane (4) and back uphill (5) to Market Place with C17 'Talbot' on blocked arcade; then green (6), down to nice sharp edge of town (7); back past shell doorway (8), Gothick church and timberframe 'Bell' (9) on cast-iron columns. Finally from 5 gables on loggia (10), splendid largely C17 curving Long Street to warehouses with cupola (11).

Oxfordshire

Oxford is not covered, being a historic city. *Banbury*, despite forced high growth, is worth exploring from its Market Place—as are the urban villages of *Deddington* and *Eynsham, Dorchester-on-Thames* and *Burford* (see page 74) with fine main streets. The attractive little towns selected show a great variety of materials, from the Georgian brick of *Thame, Henley, Abingdon* and *Wallingford* (*Wantage* and *Faringdon* are good around their market places), to the Cotswold stone houses and stone slate roofs of *Chipping Norton* and *Woodstock*.

Henley-on-Thames (1883): characteristic Georgian brick purple/red or red/yellow plus some timberframe. From bridge: brick inn with pedimented stables (1)—in yard, 1400s house; stucco and redbrick almshouses (2); brick and stucco—three with pilasters (3), medieval 'White Hart' with courtyard, curious first-floor brick windows (4), stucco hotel (5). Widens—brick pilasters and timberframe (6), pediment (7) to Town Hall and bow and bay windows (8); Georgian plus 1900s oriel, stucco and little terrace (9).

Loop to N. Commercial with pedimented Assembly Room (10) with pilasters; grand redbrick/stucco house, 12-bay terrace. Widens uphill with excellent Georgian houses: left, ironwork and window with fantop (11), timberframe 'Bear', 4 Venetian windows, two 3-storey bow windows; right, doorway urns as capitals (12). Two stucco terraces (13) and beyond (14) gate lodges with Venetian windows, and (15) C19 Gothic villas like North Oxford. Back and towards river (16)—scroll doorways, pilasters, fine brewery houses (17). Along river past Victorian boathouses to (1). Finally past 1700s rectory to stucco 1840s Belgravia-like terrace (18): lower centre, pilasters, classical porches. Back to old granary range (19), minor terrace (20) and timberframe house (21).

Thame (1885): the classic broad cigar-shape one street town, with later island encroachments. With characteristic blue/grey Georgian brick houses with redbrick panels or dressings—two of them in cul-de-sac NE of church, but also many timberframe houses, usually plastered. Starting S of church, two timberframe rows (1) and C16/17 gabled Grammar School into High Street. Nice brick pair with recessed doorways (2), Georgian front plus Tudor chimneys (3), good timberframe plus 1840s stucco (4), good Georgian each side as street opens out, Venetian windows (5) near island Town Hall (since map). Attractive timberframe inns—in Buttermarket (6), and in Cornmarket with timber side oriels, opposite splendid pilastered 'Spread Eagle' (7). Then another island, and as cigar narrows, good Georgian N side—triglyph porch and carriageway (8), timberframe S side, out to fountain in garden (9).

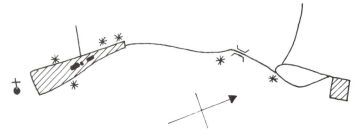

Witney: though High Street is commercialised, there are delightful greens with Georgian houses either end, and two pleasant streets off. From S to N note: in Church Green Venetian window and doorway (*), pedimented C17 crosswindows (*); islands and loggias of C17 Butter Cross and C18 Town Hall facing good shopfronts ('Angel' bows, Victorian iron); raised pavement with good stucco and two grandest houses (*)—pedimented windows, Venetian window and door, and C17 corner gables (finials). Then several nice pairs plus, on right, stucco row with rusticated pilasters, 1721 Blanket Hall (*), Gibbs windows; over bridge 1900s mill and pilastered house (tripartite doorway), courtroom, C17 gabled (*).

Chipping Norton (1885): several Baroque houses (influence of Blenheim?) and a nice plan with an irregular central space, sloping, with trees: 1730 segmental windows (1), 'White Hart' aprons above windows (2) and delicate 1780s (Venetian window, fantopped recesses), several pilastered—one with frieze (3); Venetian windows next to pedimented window and ovals (4). Nice stone rows, near Guildhall (5) with medieval openings; gabled C17 almshouses (6) with strapwork gateway. Round island Town Hall (portico) crude windowtops of 'Fox' (7), even quoins (8), to good frontage (9): 2-storey bay windows, 5-bay with even quoins (school wings), fluted pilasters and round openings. s past Gibbs doorway and round recesses (10), stone rows and C17 mullions (11) to 'Bell'.

Woodstock: at the gates of Blenheim Palace—hence some strange Baroque houses. Explore largely Georgian stone-built streets w of A34 with many fine houses and shopfronts (bow or bay windows—sometimes several stories) and characteristic flat doortops on cast-iron brackets. From island Town hall note, w: pilasters and curved eaves of 'Bear', cobbles, trees, Georgian redbrick beside pilasters, ovals near gatepiers, surprise of gateway. E: Ipswich (Oxford) style window glazing opposite redbrick hotel. SE: tall pedimented window (top with horseman), carved bargeboards. In Oxford

Street (A34) Venetian bay window over Venetian shopfront, pilasters, shell doortop, almshouse terrace, Baroque palace gates.

Abingdon (1883): many historic houses—timberframe, usually plastered like Oxford, and Georgian redbrick (some with even quoins) and stucco; but blight and redevelopment—a dreary new street (1), better library scheme (2) beside Inner Ring Road (3). From cobbled Market Place (4) with superb 1680s Town Hall, first to river: nice little courtyard (5)—loggia, recesses; timberframe inn yard; converted gaol (6); to abbey remains (7) and back through gateway (8). Then past C17 gabled 'Lion', double bow shopfront with frieze (9), to fine Georgian houses (10)—fantopped windows, and (11)—twirly windowtops (little urns) with fine stable yard (Venetian window); good stucco chapel (12), to delightful almshouses (13).

Then from (10) past C17 gabled row to fine 1722 house (14) with twirly windowtops; through (2) to fine timberframe C18 house (15) with segmental doorway; past several timberframe (16). Finally superb curving street (17) to church spire. On left, grand Georgian behind gatepiers, segmental doorways; on right, pineapple on balustrade, stone pair with ironwork, pilasters, 1732 with heads in windowtops; good range ending with stone oriel window (18). Round five-aisled church, delightful courtyard formed by three sets of almshouses: C15–17 with timber cloisterwalk, 1718 brick with giant arches including balconies, 1717 redbrick with pedimented centre.

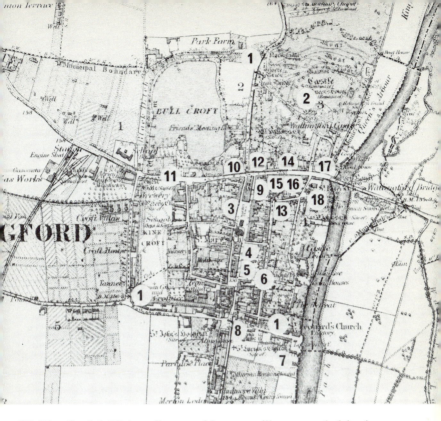

Wallingford (1883): a Saxon grid-town still surrounded by its earth defences (1), including site of later Norman castle (2). Has a characteristic Georgian purplebrick with redbrick dressings. Start at Market Place: island 1670s Town Hall on sturdy columns with Venetian window, as has house (3) near neo-Egyptian pilasters. Past church: pediment and more Venetian windows (4); corner quoins (5) and good houses behind (6); Elizabethan house (7); almshouses with Gothick glazing (8), facing little green. Back to pedestrian street (9): keystones, medieval gables with pendants, ironwork. To c18 house (10) opposite new arcade, to good houses (11): pilasters, Doric porches, c17 flintwork; and defences.

Finally best street: timberframe corner, pilasters (12), overhanging inn; up street to good houses (13)—one stone; stables with cupola behind stucco house, stone with recesses (14); c16 overhang (15) with stone steps; grandest house (16) with pilasters middle and ends, aprons, urns, fine doorway; to castle house gates (17) and fine detached house (18)—yellowbrick to lane, stone to river.

Somerset

An extensive and varied county with almost every town worth exploring. *Bath* (now in county of Avon) is not covered, being a historic city. At the other extreme are several delightful urban villages: *Bruton* with fine High Street plus packhorse bridge and abbey buttresses; *Somerton* with fine stone houses from Market Place with islands, up tree-lined Broad Street; *Langport* good past Town Hall uphill to church and chapel over arch; *Axbridge* with good Market Place (spectacular 1500s timberframe); *Crewkerne*, excellently stone-built, with good central space round Town Hall; *Ilminster* good from central Market Hall E, N and W past and round cruciform church; and on extreme W, *Dunster* with fine long street curving below castle to Market Cross. Of the larger towns: *Wincanton* has many good Georgian houses; *Chard* has a good mixed main street up and over the hill; *Glastonbury* has good houses opposite abbey, and good street from here to octagonal Market Cross, and right past church; and *Shepton Mallet* has C15 timber Shambles and stone Market Cross, many C17–18 houses on slopes of steep valley, good new infill.

Frome (1886): a delightful stone-built town in a steep valley, noteworthy for its many late C17 (gables) and C18 clothiers' houses. Explore at least from Market Place (1) past Bluecoat pediment and cupola (2) to house with pedimented windows (3), along river to 1700s terrace beyond (4) with hood doorways. Then pedestrian street (5): central conduit, timberframe, to good group W of church and cobbled C17/18 street (6)—Venetian windows; back past 1707 chapel (7) with eared arched windows. Then narrow steep winding street with raised pavements (8) to pedimented house (set back), Tuscan colonnade, nice terrace (9). Pleasant streets (10). To N: late C17 house (11) with crosswindows; on to

strange decayed C17 area (12) with gaps and new housing *or* down
lane (13) to good C18 houses (14) near new shopping precinct.

Wells (1887): a delightful little cathedral city. First down C14
planned street (1) to fine houses in Liberties: buttresses (2) plus
shell doorway; C19 and 1713 schools with cross windows,
pediments; Georgian with bay windows and Venetian doorway;
7-bay with recessed centre; medieval porch and buttresses (3);
1700s, Georgian with porch on square columns, advanced centre
and porch (both pilastered) and C17 manor (4). Then NE along
good street (5): medieval door, bow windows, pair with hood
doorways, mixed materials, C17 mullions out to 1682 house (6);
back to shell doorway (7) and sharp edge of town.

Loop into town from Market Place (8): pedimented 1779 Town
Hall, Tuscan colonnade with triglyph, stone/stucco row (buttresses, bay windows), C17 timberframe gables. Pleasant mixed
High Street with early C19 Bristol-style stone (often pilastered,
one with Gothick tops), plus recessed arch, stucco pilasters of
'Star', columned bank groundfloor, curved keystones (9); two
tripartite Venetian windows (10) and ogive bay window; C19 with
verandah (11). Then redbrick pilastered terrace (12), 'City Arms'
courtyard (13), C15 doorway (14), Gothick doors (15), Georgian
stucco (16), C15 almshouses (17) with gabled porch and sedilia
facing church. Finally good Georgian streets and houses: by (18)
to pilastered chapel (19) and little stucco terrace (20); good group
(21) with Gibbs doorway, up to segmental windows at fork and
nice sharp edge (22); back by street (23) with gateway, double
bowfront, ironwork, C17 oriel/bay window.

Bridgwater (1887): a redbrick early C18 port, with attractive street pattern and spaces, especially round church: good group (1) of Georgian with stone surrounds, classical chapel, medieval chimneybreast, and round splendid 1830s columned rotunda and market hall (2). To the Priory (3) with pilasters at front, Venetian window at back; down (4) to good streets: with C17 gable and shell hood (5), and with chapel shell door and Venetian window (6). To nice Georgian pair (7) with curving balconies facing river; group with 1840s infirmary porch (8); fine house (9) with aprons, pilasters, Gibbs doorway. Line of defences E of river?

Back down modern and Georgian street (10)—view of pedimented County Court (11)—to Victorian stone classical and another Venetian window (12). Then round rotunda to 'Royal Clarence' with columned porch, covered arcade and classical 1865 Town Hall (13). NE to Georgian square (14): keystones, pedimented doorways, nice balconies, one side (15) rebuilt behind. Into superb street (16) laid out in 1720s: eaves curving up, stone segmental surrounds, elaborate doorways. Finally to quay and good group (17)—pilastered pub, converted warehouses; on to climax of 1730 mansion (18)—rusticated pilasters, stone centre, pavilions with Venetian windows. To N attractive cobbles and warehouses of disused canal area.

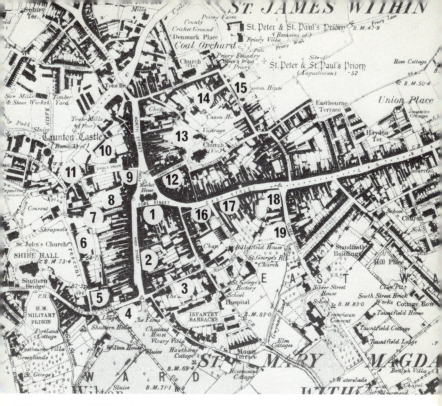

Taunton (1888): nice plan with triangular market place outside castle precinct, but much bad redevelopment. Beside fine 1770s Market House is a good frontage (1): stucco pilasters, c19 stone bank, round recesses, medieval stone door and overhanging timberframe (gables, 1578). First a loop down pedestrianised street (2)—with a fine doorway, to park gates, good group with advanced centre (3), back past stucco (4) to huge columned porch (5) and brick crescent (6) with curving balconies and rounded openings, like Exeter; back along 1900s road with contrasting Art College and Library (7) and c16 school (8).

Then 3 sallies, to mostly Georgian houses and chapels—many pilastered. Through gateway (9) into castle area—castellated Gothick hotels, 1495 gateway to nice courtyard (10) with shell doorway, good stucco villa (11)—beyond bus station! Then formal street (12) with pedimented doorways to church tower, by lane (13) to more mixed (14) with octagonal chapel, little terrace; and (15) with keystones, big surrounds. Finally E: nice stucco curve and hotel (16) with alley; then (17) redbrick with advanced centre; c17 almshouses with 9 chimneys (18); and up street to pedimented centre with wings (19).

Wiltshire

A marvellous varied county with many attractive little towns. *Lacock* and *Corsham* (see Gloucestershire) are fine urban villages (recent high growth at Corsham). *Warminster* and *Wootton Bassett* have good main streets; *Chippenham* and *Calne*, despite redevelopment, are worth exploring—as is *Westbury*; and *Highworth* has surprising grand early C18 houses. *Trowbridge*, while not as good, can be combined with another stone clothiers' town, Frome. It has blight and gaps, but a complex plan—Castle and Court streets mark castle site developed in 1814, with impressive mills; and many fine C18 houses, capped by the incredible palazzi of Fore Street and the Parade.

Wilton: a small town, once the county town, with a mixture of thatch, timberframe, redbrick, stone and stucco. From nice Market Place and nearby islands (C18 Town Hall quoins, band, ruined church): N to little bridge; S to bridge (gables with Venetian window) with good detached houses beyond; W grand pilasters, church, to bend by medieval hospital; and best E to green, good C18 hotel and house (set back), by gates to Wilton House.

Salisbury (1887): has perfect cathedral exterior and close, classic C13 grid plan of 'chequers', and a wealth of medieval timberframe, C17 and Georgian houses—many tilehung. Also new Inner Ring Road (9). Despite grid, I attempt a tour: along E–W streets, exploring N–S from them. Through S gate of close (1), terrace and corner conglomerate (2) to medieval hospital (3) and bridge. Round walls of close to timberframe inn and pedimented window (4) and grand hotel portico. Up fine street (5)—and to C17 friary buildings (6), C17/18 inn (7), past timberframe oriels on scroll brackets (8) to IRR (9) and nice Georgian (10). Up (11) to splendid 1700s Trinity hospital (12) with courtyard, carparks, truncated high-level road; grand 7-bay and new carpark (13) opposite timberframe and Georgian; fine houses and medieval C18 complex (14) by the river.

Then good Georgian to gate of close (15), elaborate timberframe (16) masking new shopping centre, to marvellous intricate gabled area round St Thomas' (17) and Poultry Cross (18): islands and encroachments, plus the present Market Place. Then (19) past pilastered houses to site of castle gate (20); (21), (22), past almshouses (23) to fine C18 house (24) with Gibbs surrounds everywhere. (25) to (26)—gaps, to C15 inn/hall (27), (28), C14 (29) on corner of Market Place. Along (30): new shopping tucked away

(31), keystones, c18 front/c17 side (32), c17 almshouses (33), to return past good infill (34), (35) with early c19 brewery, 1820s inn with timberframe courtyard (36).

Devizes (1889): the curving streets, with a wealth of 1700–1840 buildings, form concentric rings from the former castle (1), the first market place (2) and streets developing outside the line (3-14-27) of the castle bailey, which was subsequently 'colonised' with the second and present market place (4).

Round (4): elaborate 1740s doctor's house (5), good inn and shopfronts, arcade with clocktower (6); islands, fine Cheese Hall (7) with columns, pediment; recessed columns (8), stone and stucco 'Bear', Corn Exchange with figure (9); good group (rustications) to shell door and grand redbrick (10) behind gatepiers. Then group (11) with Soanian pilasters opposite tilehung timberframe, little Gothick school; grand redbrick opposite court portico (12); canal, with Rennie's 29 locks down to left.

From (7): timberframe overhang with pilasters opposite (13); pedestrianised (14) with terrace, quoins and Gothick glazing, pilasters fluted and paired. Past good corner (2) to grand redbrick house (15) with gatepiers and ironwork; Georgian factory opposite good group (16). Back past fine 'Castle' to group (17) with C15 timberframe to columned shopfront (18). In street (19): redbrick with bands opposite little square with arcade and ironwork, 4 + 3 + 4-bay with Soanian details. Grand stone house (20) with stables, bow window; good frontage (21) with rusticated terrace.

Back to (7) and group opposite: rounded openings, purplebrick with rusticated pilasters, timberframe (22), pilastered windows (Gibbs, pedimented). Delightful area round splendid Town Hall, with overhanging timberframe up alley towards (7), and with pilasters, segmental windows (23). Then grand segmental centre (24) and fine street to (25): some timberframe but mostly Georgian (tripartite door, Venetian windows), plus similar stretch (26), and terrace with garlands (27).

Malmesbury (1889): attractive stone and stucco hill town round Norman abbey church. Start at splendid 1500s Market Cross (1). Georgian stone with garlanded doorway opposite old water tower (2); huge c16 Abbey House (3). Then loop: tower over c15 roof through arch (4), to square and segmental windows plus arcade (5), pedimented centre (6); down steep lane (7) to nice space, c17 almshouses (8), late c18 silk mill. Then stone cottages (9) to c17 5-bay (10) plus 3-bay (shell door, balustrade); triglyph door and bow window (11); quoins, Gothick shopfront, gabled dated 1671 (12); left, square bay windows (13); right elaborate Georgian redbrick. Finally nice street round churchspire (14), 'Bell' and Gothick chapel; Georgian pilastered door, ironwork (15); to pediment (16). Behind, stone cottage area (17), to Horsefair (18) with c17 gabled row.

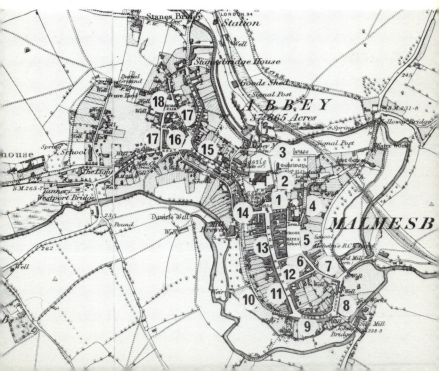

Bradford-on-Avon (1889): a delightful stone-built town in a steep valley, with C17 gabled and mullioned houses, C18 with big window surrounds, segmental tops, and/or pilasters (some rusticated). Three sallies from bridge (1). First to 'Swan' (2) with circular and Venetian windows in good group; Gibbs doorway (3) and C16 corner: splendid mill (4); Bristol-style house (5) with pilastered centre and balustrade; pedimented centre (6), door and windows; church and Saxon chapel; 1697 row and C17 with frieze doorway (7). Up to: pediment with oval (8) opposite 2 + 7 + 2 terrace; nice frontage (9) with a shell doorway; C17 rows (10); to terraces (11), curving with end bay windows, pedimented doorways, and pilgrim chapel (12). Back down main road — hood doorway in good group (13), exposed timberframe up lane (14).

Secondly up curving street: varying windowtops (15) between good lanes to chapel (16) and Manor House (17) with urns; pilasters and Gibbs windows (18) and good Georgian (19). Past loggia (20) to bay/Venetian window, two fine houses with segmental windows, stucco villa with verandah (21), C17 Hall (22). Thirdly to fine frontage (23): twirly windowtop, Soanian pilasters, round to chapels (24) and nice houses up lane (25); grand

house (26) with good garden details and Bristol-style side; Georgian (27)—recesses, keystones, curly doortop; to 1700s almshouses (28).

Marlborough (1889): a classic superb wide main street, with fine Georgian houses—basically brick but many tilehung; several Venetian (one with bay) and tripartite windows. From castle mound and huge early C18 mansion (1) in College: pilasters (2); Gothick windows (3) behind new shops; houses and inns to river (4); colonnade (5). Delightful area round island church and Town Hall (6): uphill, pilastered curve (7), timberframe and excellent Georgian (8), as in attractive green (9), with one stone house. More Georgian up (10), down (11) to early-C19 villa (12).

6 Wales

Despite the Welsh names and language everywhere visible, there are no obvious 'Welsh' architectural characteristics, as there are 'Scottish' ones in Scotland. Like Northern Scotland, it was a largely poor, mountainous land, and the early towns were almost all 'planted'—in Wales mostly by Edward I beside his castles. *Cardiff*, a C19 growth town and not on CBA list, was only made the 'capital' of Wales in 1955. So compared with Scotland, there are no 'lowlands', and no historic capital city.

Nonetheless, outside industrial South Wales, Caernarvonshire and the Wrexham/Flint area, almost all Welsh towns are delightful small market towns worth exploring—including some not mentioned later such as *Machynlleth* and *Bala*. They have fewer Georgian or historic buildings than in England, but they still function as country market towns, feeding on and serving their surrounding rural areas.

Stone is commonly used, but also stucco, usually painted white, often contrasted with window frames and doorways painted black—what I call Welsh black-and-white Georgian—to be distinguished from black-and-white timberframe 'magpie' houses. These types are also common in the English Pennines and the Border Counties of Cheshire, Shropshire, Herefordshire, and in Monmouthshire—once English, now Gwent in Wales.

Welsh town names: where the Welsh name is different from the name in English, both are given. Where there is only a difference in spelling (e.g. Conwy) only the English version is given.

Glamorgan

Cowbridge/Y Bont-faen: apparently just a good, largely Georgian main street. Explore 100 yards E of 1830s Town Hall (clocktower, recessed arches); best houses to w: ogive door arch opposite 2 high Venetian windows; stone with ground floor rustication; out to fine classical porch. But s down Church Street is a medieval gate and stretch of town wall.

Dyfed

Like the best beaches, the most famous historic towns are in the old Pembrokeshire—usually with castles, as has *Narberth*

(Arberth), with an intricate street plan and pleasant spaces (best houses in St James's Street). *Fishguard* (Abergwaun) has a fine main street down SE from its Town Hall. *St David's* (Tyddewi) is a village/city with a huge grey cathedral (and bishop's palace) dramatically situated in a hollow and approached at tower level through gateway; little townscape to compete with this, though pleasant round village cross and down lane past chapel.

Haverfordwest/Hwllffordd (1891): a complex and varied historic town on a hill. Follow main street from bridge (1) up to magnificent church (2) past fine coaching inns. Two good loops. First: below (2) to little square with good inn (3) and two-storey Regency ironwork (4); to attractive area round church (5); up to the castle/gaol/museum (6); round past two Regency terraces (7) to Old Bridge (8); returning along nice street to little square (9). Second: from (2) to Market Hall (10); along Hill St with grand Georgian houses to green (11); to attractive area with gardens overlooking river (12) round church; return past good houses and high pavement (13).

Tenby/Dinbych-y-pysgod (1890): outstanding for its combination of walled historic town and seaside resort. Follow the walls round, past corner (1) and unusual barbican 'five arches' (2). Then explore every street within walled town. Best (3), and the spine from hotels (4), past classical Town Hall to spacious church by central space, Tudor Merchant's house (5), C18 inns, to grand Regency houses and terrace (6): slatehung sides, stucco pilasters

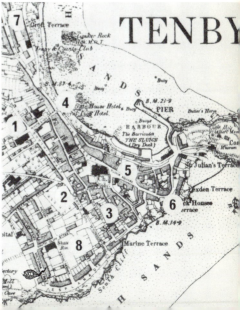

on front, precariously supported by cast-iron columns above cliffs. Most attractive round harbour and to castle. Outside the walls: Regency houses quite far N (7); to W attractive Victorian seaside area (8) of classical doorways and double 3-storey bowfronts—like Aberystwyth.

Pembroke/Penfro (1869): a long, thin, one-street castle town on a superb site, with much of its town wall visible from S. From bridge (1), good street up past medieval stone houses/Westgate (2), along ridge past coaching inns, island, good Melbourne house (3) and second church.

In the old Carmarthenshire, *Carmarthen* (Caerfyrddin) is now severed by new roads from its bridge crossing, but has some good streets near castle (Georgian Quay Street), with Regency houses out of town beside column. *Llandeilo* is good down Carmarthen Street to and round church, and to bridge; and so is most of *Newcastle Emlyn* (Castellnewydd Emlyn).

Llandovery/Llanymddyfri: from church, good main street (castle behind) to islands round Town and Market Halls, with cross—whence runs nice Stone Street.

Laugharne/Lacharn: an attractive urban village, Dylan Thomas' 'Llareggub'. From estuary and view of castle, explore area round the cross (The Grist), and walk past medieval stone house, Town Hall, to fine Georgian houses (3-storey bow window) next to raised pavement.

There are four attractive towns in the old Cardiganshire, plus the urban village of *Tregaron*.

Cardigan/Aberteifi: attractive warehouses, boats, textures by river, and superb curving High Street up from it, with narrowing of street, up to Guildhall (2-storey C19 Gothic crypt/market); good down St Mary's Street—past nasty gap for new road—to church.

Lampeter/Llanbedr Pont Steffan: good early C19 buildings in High Street (stone terrace, old bank and inns with fine porches) and charming C19 neo-Tudor University College quadrangle.

Aberaeron (1889): a delightful little early C19 grid-planned port, with its harbour forming central space. Stucco terraces (grander 3-storey on corners, 2-storey between) extend well up main A487 both sides of bridge, round Alban Square, and along both sides of river.

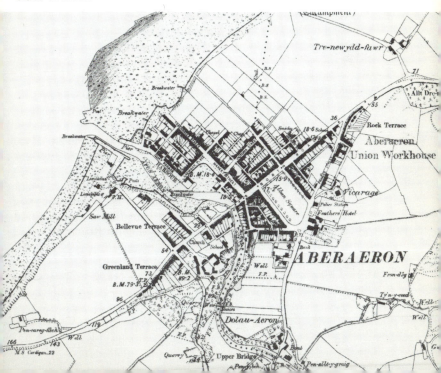

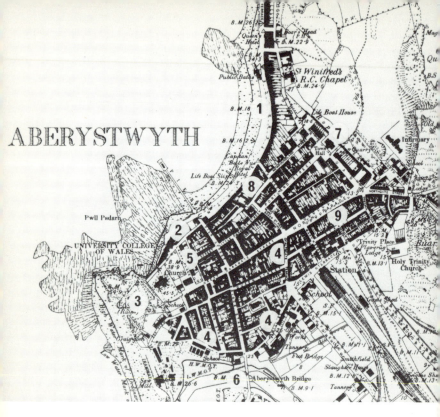

Aberystwyth (1887): Regency and early Victorian stucco houses (3-storey bow or bay windows, classical doorways) interspersed with earlier C18 houses (good doorways). A long, grand seafront (1), the splendid C19 Gothic University College (2) by contrast giving an appropriately dense and irregular medieval air near the castle (3). Note line of walls (4). Excellent streets and houses: round the church (5); from the pier to the bridge (6); from (5) to Town Hall (7)—and towards front (8); and from (7) towards attractive wide North Parade (9).

Gwynedd

In Anglesey, *Holyhead* (Caergybi) has a pleasant High Street, and C4 stone fort round church; but C19 Custom House, Port Offices and Doric arch are now swallowed up in car ferry terminal.

Beaumaris (1888/9): Edward I castle *bastide*, C18 county town, later a seaside resort. Along seafront: half square of white houses (1), good ironwork, 'Bulkeley Arms'; splendid stone 1830s terrace, raked back from its pedimented and pilastered centre; humbler terrace (2), looking out to green lawns by the sea. Past C17 courthouse to main Castle Street, mostly stucco, many Georgian black and white inns: left, stone 'Bulkeley Arms' (3) and old Town Hall on arcade; right, redbrick, inn with 1766 rainwaterheads, C15 timberframe (4). Good loop up to church and little pilasters opposite round windows beneath pediments (5); remains of town walls behind 'Sailor's Return' (6); to C19 brick street with trees betweeen gate-piers (7); back round past impressive C19 gaol (8).

Then the old Caernarvonshire with 5 planned towns; medieval Conway and mid C19 Llandudno nearby make a delightful contrasting pair to explore in one day.

Llandudno: a spacious mid-Victorian seaside resort laid out by Lord Mostyn in 1849. An obelisk marks where the avenue from Conway Bay curves gently round on either side (classical doorways) to join seafront; along it is a grand terrace, with pilasters and an attic storey marking hotels each end, coming forward with classical porch at centre. Then higher, and later, hotel with Scots baronial eaves, modern infill with 3-storey bay windows, 'Hydro'. Inland to gardens, trees and main shopping street with cast-iron arcades—following it to oldest (early C19) houses, beneath Great Orme.

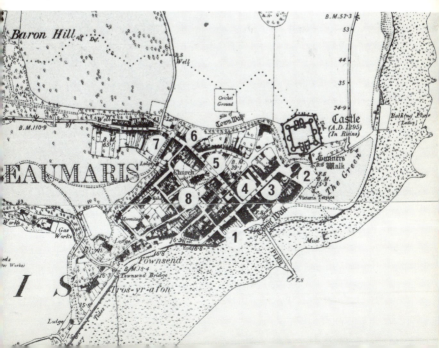

Conway (1891): another Edward I *bastide* and notable for its complete town walls, with drum towers—and hilly like Carcassonne. Visit castle—views of town walls and Telford's and Robert Stephenson's bridges; follow walls along quay with C19 classical pub (1), under arches round to (2)—the start in Berry Street of an incredible heady walk along walls, high over roads and terraces, up to highest corner and descending at (3). It is worth returning to (2), and walking same stretch from outside, past (7). Enter elaborate Upper Gate (3) and follow walls inside, past C19 pub, into railway yard to see Mill Gate (4), and back to castle.

Explore Castle Street with classical black and white houses (2-storey bay windows, little pilasters next to window), 1589 pub and C15 house (5). And High Street, with grand stone Plas Mawr, and Georgian Mansion House. Into square (6), to Regency pub and gate (7); returning past stone and stucco terraces earlier seen from above (8), classical shopfront, and side of Plas Mawr.

Caernarvon (1891): county town and *bastide*, its walls, compared with Conway, enclosing a smaller level area, with many more good houses and attractive vistas down the streets. First walk round town (and castle) walls from outside: along the sea, barbican West Gate (1), Regency former custom-house (now hotel) with good ironwork, and church fitted into corner. Facing castle, pub with groundfloor Ionic pillars, classical portico of 1863 Court House (2).

Then explore grid of streets in detail. E of (1), High Street largely Georgian—of stucco, brick and stone: keystones, pillared shopfronts, ogive glazing, good doorways. Then some points to look for in the N–S streets, taking them from E to W in two halves, first N, then S of High Street. Georgian row and 'Black Boy'; 3-storey bay windows, white terrace houses and stone market facade (as has Hole-in-the-Wall Street to E). Georgian houses, some with 1800 rainwaterheads, bulky 1886 corner buildings; stone house with tripartite windows, 10-window terrace. Church, stone and rough-cast infill housing, good fanlights and columned doorways; two symmetrical houses with fanlights, double pilasters of Court House, C19 county offices.

Outside walled town, Castle Square (3) has brick terrace, stone classical bank, and range with fluted Corinthian pilasters. Beyond, early C19 terrace (4); behind, stone-built street with good new infill at end. Uphill to E chunky new offices with stone rubble staircases and slate roofs (5). Towards Bangor Regency houses and stone 'Royal Hotel' (6).

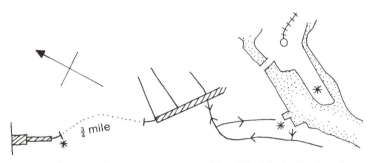

Portmadoc & Tremadoc: created by Mr Madocks in 1810s. Portmadoc has become a thriving market and holiday town—of dark stone and stucco, its High Street (largely spoilt but good inns) between pleasant residential streets. Do loop shown: to little half-square (*) facing harbour (good houses, inns, harbour buildings and 4-storey warehouses); take lane up to road with attractive terraces to left and right, and views over good holiday development on old slate wharf (*) to the mountains. Tremadoc, inland, has never grown beyond its original dark stone buildings round the spacious square, with Town Hall and hotel, under huge cliffs—like the extraordinary Montenegrin capital of Cetinje. To s good new infill, grand Regency house with cast-iron porch and elaborate window lintels, and white Tuscan chapel portico (*).

Clwyd

The old Flintshire has two good streets rising pleasantly up to church and cathedral respectively at *Mold* (Yr Wyddgrug) and *St Asaph* (Llanelwy), stone cottages near the castle at *Rhuddlan* and nice 1816 brick terraces at the centre of *Holywell* (Treffynon); but the best two towns are those that follow, in the old Denbighshire.

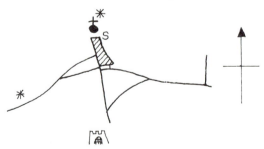

Ruthin: good houses of timber, stone, stucco and brick. Start from Market Place on hill, with medieval timberframe and 'Castle

Hotel'—half Tudor chimneys and huge roof punched through by 3 rows of dormers, half C18 brick with aprons under windows. First church (extension with Gothick windows) and C18 house nearby (*). From 1401 timberframe on island: Well Street descends past curved stone 1825 chapel facade, Georgian 'Wynstay Arms', C17 red stone Plas Coch, Georgian brick house and shopfront, to nice railway terrace; and excellent street past C18 stucco inn on loggia, several timberframe to gates of the castle/hotel—whence lane down castellated stone wall. From Market Place attractive streets join to reach good stone house and massive gaol (*) next to river.

Denbigh/Dinbych (1879): Vale Street (1) leads up, with grand Georgian houses (stone left, brick with keystones right), to spacious High Street (2) plus Crown Square up to Town Hall (3); 1570s house, row supported by pillars and others on arcades. Climb steeply to left through Burgesses Gate (4) into strange, empty hilltop area of deserted medieval walled town (stone cottages and walls); and to castle (5), and ruined Leicester church (6), near good stretch of town wall. Those with energy left can sally out from High Street: down to grey Georgian house (7); or to C18 houses and cottages, downhill in areas (8) and (9).

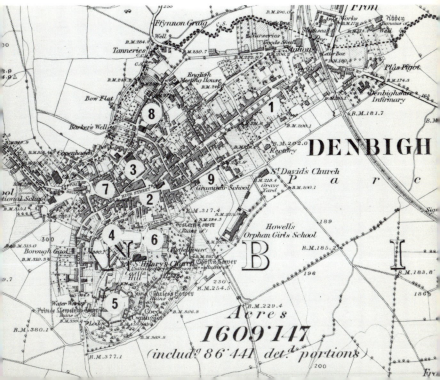

Powys

The old Radnorshire has 3 places to explore. *Knighton* (Trefyclo) is a market town, with medieval plan, building up nicely to clocktower and up behind to top of hill; good early C19 houses down street to church. *Llandrindod Wells* is by contrast a spa town spaciously laid out 1890–1910 in confident unmellowed redbrick—with avenues, squares and gardens. *Presteigne* (Llanandras) is an attractive little town, its main street good w of prominent timberframe house. At right angles, fine Broad Street—cobbled, spacious, C17 and C18 plus the columns and pilasters of 1829 Assize Courts.

The old Montgomeryshire has 4 places worth exploring—mostly Georgian redbrick, but with some stucco, timberframe and occasionally stone. At attractive *Llanidloes* sally out from 1600s Market Hall, down four streets nicely closed visually by houses at ends and under building to C19 terrace along river. At *Newtown* (Y Drenewydd), explore from clocktower: NE, SE to ironwork above statue, NW to interesting Georgian industrial area over bridge.

Welshpool/Y Trallwng (1886): the attractive former county town. Towards Station, detached Georgian houses (1); canal aqueduct (2), lock and warehouse (3); into town, brick range with recessed arches and inn with two classical doorways (4). In main shopping street: 3 pilastered houses, New Street (5) with chapel lancets and stone group; Town Hall (6) and good shopfront in street at side, opposite stucco house dated 1816. Street curves pleasantly past good houses—one stone, several half-timbered (some only on sides) to stone cottage range (7) at top. Back to (4), fine shopfronts with 6 fluted columns (8). Georgian houses and

warehouses up to church (9); 5-storey stone mill building in carpark behind (4); out to stucco villa setback, and slate-hung house of 1836, opposite early C19 terrace (10) and 'Powis Arms'.

Montgomery/Trefaldwyn (1885): though historic county town and smallest Municipal Borough before re-organisation, now Georgian urban village, well within walls of 1220s 'New Town' — as map shows. In grand, wide street (1): fine Town Hall, 3-storey bay windows, keystones. Out past nice row (2), to Dutch gable on line of walls (3) and church. From Town Hall: up behind to Castle (4); and past Venetian window in gabled wing and timberframe cottages (5) to pleasant green (6) and extraordinary Piranesian gateway and gaol (7).

The old Breconshire has three good places to explore.

Hay-on-Wye/Gelli Gandryll (1888): a lively market town, famous for its secondhand bookshops; an intricate medieval plan, and Georgian houses of stone and stucco, many with canopies over doorways. Explore from bridge to street (1) with cobbles and best houses (big stucco one with keystones) to little clocktower, and up pedestrian street to Cheese Market on arcade (2), pillared Butter Market. Explore nearby streets, with attractive pilastered shopfronts. Past ruined castle plus C17 addition (3), out to pedimented 'Swan' (4) and almshouses; back past pedimented house (5) to remains of town walls (6).

Brecon/Aberhonddu (1888): a lively and most attractive town; Georgian and early Victorian stucco houses, often with pilasters (on street corners), good doorways and classical shopfronts. Explore intricate area within medieval defences (existing walls s side) in detail. In central space (1) a little terrace faces fine frontage: pediment and rustications; hotel porch; 3 Venetian windows. Out to site of gate (2): Regency house; bulging Doric columns of Shire Hall; curved corner with pilastered windows. Further out (3) houses dated 1774 and with quoins everywhere; good houses both sides (nice iron balconies) out to massive Victorian barracks. Back to (2) and left: house with curious niche, good railings, medieval/C17 stone house forming corner (4), to twirly windowtops and timberframe with bargeboards (5). Then little terraces left (6) and down to right (7)—Gibbs surrounds; over bridge to good houses—pediment (8), and medieval school chapel.

Back to centre, pedimented Guild Hall (9), and street behind: 1700s with bracketed eaves (10); tripartite windows; stone surrounds; and grand C18 *redbrick* (11), with keystones, railings, rusticated doorway. Finally a long loop: past covered market and bow windows (12), to castle remains in hotel (13); old stone gaol (14), good corner group, up to Priory Church (15), now cathedral; down path to river (16). Ending with The Struet: left, two-storey bay window; grand house (17) with patterned eaves and triglyph doorway; right, terrace with Ionic details, doorway with grapes, redbrick with Venetian windows, pediment.

Crickhowell/Crughywel: an urban village of stone and stucco. Main A40: nice bend, good inns and shopfronts, castellated stone walls. From cross, excellent High Street. On right: terrace from curve, Town Hall, lane to churchyard. On left: symmetrical pediments, minor terrace and castle tower up street, two fine early C18 houses (keystones, Venetian window). Past good house at end, Gothick windows and nice shopfront down to medieval bridge.

Gwent

Formerly Monmouthshire and in England. *Usk* is a pleasant little town, and *Tredegar* has a Victorian planned area centred on rondpoint with column/clocktower of 1858.

Monmouth/Trefynwi (1886): most attractive, with many Georgian stucco houses, often with quoins and/or keystones. Pilasters round central square (1)—on row, 'Beaufort Arms', Shire Hall, beside which a good group down to two pedimented houses (2) with oval, Gothick tracery, ironwork. Up past shell door to castle ruins and fine 1673 house (3). Past timberframe and grand 'White Swan' to gates and urns (4) of churchyard. Facing it: good shopfront (and heads in top windows), pub with strange columns in porch, first-floor (5); pair with caryatids; Gothick door behind columns, and fine 7-bay house (6). To N good doorways (7), 1740s and Gothick houses. Along river past pair (8) to classical Market Hall (9) opposite two amazingly metropolitan terraces.

Then down to fortified bridge, commercialised but good houses on left—grand setback behind railings (10), Venetian windows in

recesses; pub with medieval stonework, opposite at bottom, restored 4-bay house (11). Good frontage (12) over bridge (Gothick glazing, pilasters), to house with battlemented wing (13). Zigzag across area (14) with more pilasters and pediments to fine Georgian street (15): scroll double window between pilasters, segmental windows, decorated bands. Finally green, tollhouse and fine redbrick house (16).

Abergavenny/Y Fenni (1886): an attractive irregular plan, many Georgian painted houses. Good curving street up hill (1): left, grand 'Angel', bank with railings, ogive window in pediment; right, pilasters, stone arches, Town Hall with green roof (2). *Loop A:* past house with keystones (3); round castle (4) to two classical chapels (5); returning down good street (6)—insignia of 'Kings Head', Georgian row (rustications), c17 woodwork at first floor and six boars' heads at eaves. *Loop B:* from (2) past colonnade to minor and grander (7) Georgian, with four contrasting porches, back by priory church (8) and tithe barn. Beyond (2) main street curves pleasantly—left, house and tower; but more commercialised, though symmetrical pediments above fascias (9), widening at fork. To N pedimented house (10). To W, c19 classical houses with Gothick one at junction (11); similar residential area to S (12).

Chepstow/Casgwent (1886): famous castle; fine remains of town wall; one long historic street, sometimes split. Outside gate (1): exuberant neo-1700s Edwardian 'King's Head', out to good house with frieze over door (2); uphill pediment, nice shopfront (3) opposite pilastered pub, little Ionic pilasters on doorway, to stucco houses—one with Gothick glazing (4). Inside gate: c18 houses and walls with drumtowers (5). Down main street (nastily commercialised): Regency island bank; best fork left past Gothick glazing (shopfront, house with bands), to bow window with nice iron canopy (6)—with pilasters (7) across municipalised Square. Splits into three: cobbles and bow windows left; stucco middle; best past rusticated hotel on right (8)—to almshouses with Victorian bargeboards (9).

Then to church (Norman priory nave), minor Georgian area (10), 1700s pedimented house with oval window (11), warehouse area by river (12), and bridges—one by Brunel (13) and handsome cast-iron (14). Finally back uphill to centre: pedimented houses and doorways (15); gap for castle (good walk round to town walls); best group—good doorway (fanlight and pilasters), delightful Regency terrace with bow windows (16), tripartite windows in recesses, c17 stone with medieval gable window, ending with 1716 almshouses (17) on corner.

7 The Welsh Border

Cheshire

Chester (1882): justly famous for its black and white (genuine C15–17 or exuberant and inventive late C19) and Georgian houses—brick (red, purple/grey); and unique for its three pedestrian systems: the famous rows (plus arcades) often with slender classical columns; the canal towing path (rocky cutting, staircase locks, junction with river); and the town walls.

First do circuit of wall, noting: fine classical gates (N, S, E and W); in NE sector, Gothick and 2-storey bow windows; NW, infirmary bay window on columns; SW, brick buttressed house plus two stucco, sallying out to Harrison's splendid classical pavilions and castle courtyard (1) and bridge (2); SE corner, two Georgian redbrick houses (one with quoins) and 6 timberframe gables on brackets. Then explore marvellously dense urban main streets (and the rows on either side) out to the gates from the Cross (3), with sallies into Georgian areas.

First, N. Pedimented stone front with Ionic columns (4), Victorian Town Hall, past interesting side of C17 'Pied Bull' (5) past Venetian doorways to tall bay window at end (6), over cutting to Hospital (pediment, cupola, curved windowtops) and C18 arcade (7). Returning, up cobbled lane to terrace (8), row with pilasters and little pediment (9), through gateway (Gothick windows) to area of Close (10).

Then E. Stone classical house, splendid C19 with tower, pedimented stucco, Dutch gable (11) opposite fine C19 classical bank (12) and 1896 gabled black and white (since map) towards cathedral. Then clock and ironwork on walls, classical bank and courtyard with columns (13), good new store jutting out—opposite ogive window and rusticated arcade (14). Good loop to river past 4 good Georgian houses: rusticated ground-floor (15), rectory with quoins (16), pilastered ground floor and doorway (17), Old Palace (18), and to Norman St John's and nice houses beyond bridge (19).

Then S. w side rows particularly attractive (twisted balusters, stone arches, bridge); into Georgian street (20)—Venetian window opposite detached pedimented house (21). Beyond church, Gothick glazing and grand stucco house (22)—central window surround, aprons; opposite, pilasters of brick and stucco (23), up Georgian street (24)—C17 gables with urns and balls, rusticated quoins, to church (25). Then twirly scroll doorway and

stone chapel (26), terrace with 3 slim doorways (27); w side terrace with ovals (28) — nice housing behind, Gothick window, short cobbled street (29) with C17 gable.

Best of all w. House with rusticated quoins and aprons, next to fine 8-bay (30); best historic timberframe (31); terrace with slim Venetian doorways (32), along new road. Finally medieval palace (33), becomes (34) Georgian redbrick (nice columned corner); to good streets with pedimented bay windows at ends plus sedan porch (35).

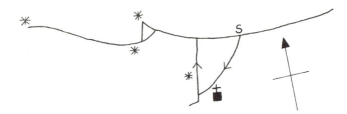

Congleton. Georgian town based on silk and cotton mills, many of whose buildings survive. From dramatic C19 Gothic Town Hall opposite timberframe 'White Lion': E past Georgian houses to timberframe dated 1671; loop with good houses to church and pilastered stucco row (*); W down nice curve to pilastered pub at end (*), round past the timberframe 'Lion and Swan' (*), to street with gaps but fine houses—one with Gibbs surrounds and one pedimented with stone quoins (*), almost at A34.

Nantwich (1888): much timberframe (after 1583 fire) and Georgian redbrick, with intricate plan. Near magnificent church (1): terrace with 3-storey bow/bay windows at ends (2), and beyond green space 4 gables with figures (3). Nearby pilastered Venetian window and first-floor quoins amid good timberframe (4). Over bridge to excellent (5)—overhanging timberframe, two grand Georgian houses (pilasters, keystones) and pedimented gateway; then more Georgian (an advanced centre, curved windowtops)—almost to Telford's canal aqueduct and basin.

Back to (3), and another timberframe (6) with carved brackets. Past columned shop and pubfronts to grand 1736 house (7)—curved window surrounds, pediment, pilasters, and Georgian street (8). E from exuberant 1910 corner (9): on left, Tuscan hotel porch, timberframe oriel window (10); right, beyond new road, round recesses (11), ogive doorway, out to 2-storey bay/bow window (12) and spectacular 1577 Churche's Mansion opposite house with fine doorway between quoined wings.

Herefordshire

A most attractive county; its unspoilt country market towns have a wealth of black and white timberframe and redbrick Georgian houses plus some stucco (often painted black and white). *Pembridge* (C16 Market House) and *Weobley* are attractive black and white urban villages, and the little towns of *Kington* (many pedimented houses) and *Bromyard* are worth exploring.

Ledbury: from island Market Hall with open ground floor, good sallies in 3 directions. First little loop up picturesque cobbled lane, past excellent overhanging timberframe, to fine church and Lower Hall (*); back to right of corner Gibbs doorway. Secondly N: left, double shopfront with triglyph frieze, shell door, Venetian window; right, pedimented with little round windows, 2-storey timberframe porch; out to redbrick rows (segmental windows) and Baptist Church (*) with recesses. Thirdly S. Good frontages along wide street W side: Victorian hospital; C14 sandstone chapel with fine roof inside; timberframe dated 1675; 'Feathers' with wooden brackets and Ionic pilasters—as also a house further on. Magnificent gabled overhanging timberframe at cross-roads; E, cottages with pedimented doors; W out to more gabled timberframe facing each other. Continuing S: opposite redbrick wall, pub with 12 tripartite windows, pedimented centre and wings out to redbrick group at nice sharp edge.

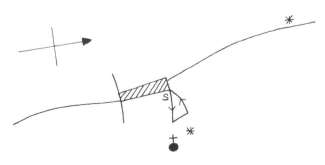

Hereford (1887): less of a close than other cathedral cities, and a controversial Inner Ring Road (1) along line of walls (remains). Three sallies recommended from pedestrian High Town (2), with Old House, market entrance opposite 1865 stucco Baroque. First to N (3). Right, nice first floor windows and balconies, pediment, neo-Egyptian pilasters; left, 1700s deep eaves. Then pilasters and good doorways (4) out to C17 courtyard, ruins, cross (5). Secondly E: bow windows facing church, Doric portico (6), to area with good doorways—on right, Town Hall, pedimented house with wings, elaborate window surrounds (7), another 1700s, tripartite windows. Then right past stucco terrace with neo-Egyptian details, to good group (8) in secluded area: behind Gothick almshouses to castle green (9), stucco house with medieval doorways (10); good street (11)—N side: ironwork, classical villa; s side: keystones (C14 hall behind). Facing cathedral: house of re-used stone and Gothick glazing up lane (12); nice mixed street to recessed corner (13); two grand houses (14). Up attractive lane (good shopfront, round windows) to (2).

Finally w. Timberframe embodied in Littlewoods (15)! Good buildings towards cathedral West Front: left, pediment and rustications, C19 bank, iron porch (16), huge columns; right, stucco with pilasters, as is pedimented hotel, and neo-Gothic library. Mixed Georgian and timberframe down to river: pilastered shopfront (17); up street to broad gables and double doorways of 1630 almshouses (18) with Venetian window opposite; beyond (1) nice terrace (19), part of late Georgian area (20); good early C18 group (21), terrace with canopies facing river (22); over medieval bridge to delightful terraces (23) and 1700s house (24) now rebuilt.

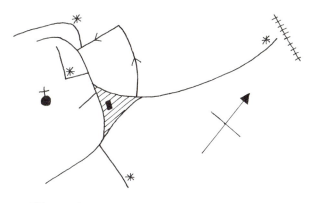

Ross-on-Wye: a hilltop town, capped by church spire. Round churchyard: prospect garden (1700s gate); Gothick sandstone 'ruins' (not town walls) opposite 'Royal Hotel' (bargeboards, ironwork); houses with Gothick doorway (*); C16 almshouse opposite good pair with Gibbs surround. Then 3 sallies from triangular sloping Market Place with C17 island Town Hall, timberframe carved brackets, recessed arches (rebuilt). First SE: inn with quoins and keystones; 8 tripartite windows on corner; down street to 1790s school (*); uphill to stone house with ovals and almshouses with Gothick glazing. Second W: pilasters (including splendid 'King's Head'), redbrick curve with balconies, C18 stone, to widening. Left, new road with 'rocks and middleagery' (Pevsner). Right, delightful old road to river: right battlements, stucco pilasters on angle (*), on left Gothick villa, bottom of school, door and windows (plus niche). Finally N: good houses (keystones, quoins) out to two early C18 houses (*) with hood doorway and a C17 gable. Good loop along Georgian street—bow and bay windows, fanlights, grand stucco house, Gothick old Gaol; to big Regency houses above river (urn over door), and back left.

Leominster (1886): start at central square (1)—stucco row, classical shopfront repeated at first floor! Across lawn, 1633 Town Hall (moved) with incredibly lavish details (2), and priory church (3). From (1) between two timberframe (4) to street with good Georgian doorways out to 1770s chapel complex (5); back past nice 1850s Gothic house (6) and out to redbrick house with quoins (7). To centre, past pedimented 'Royal Oak' to irregular crossroads (8) and splendid hotel range (9)—bay windows with blank arches, earlier segmental windows, timber-frame with bow windows. Then three right turns: heads on carriageway arches (10); 6-bay pediment, timberframe, rose window (11); timber-frame 3-gable *plastered*, dated 1673 (12); past corner diagonal bracing back to (1).

Finally N. Along pedestrian street (13) to two grand Georgian streets. Towards (3) stone chapel and grandest house (14), opposite stucco house with Corinthian porch. In Broad Street (good doorways and shopfronts): left, 7-bay with caryatid shopfront (15), tripartite windows with frieze and lion on parapet; right, fine timberframe dated 1600, pedimented window and double door, recessed groundfloor (16); at end 4 Venetian windows and Gothick fanlight (17). Then nice range to and along river, late C17 with hooded door and quoins (18), badly needed new infill, to strange house with timberframe pediment (19).

Shropshire

A varied county—hilly border country to s, into Cheshire Plain to N, with characteristic Georgian redbrick and exposed timber-frame. *Whitchurch* is worth exploring (good High Street s of church), as are smaller *Market Drayton* (Butter Cross on Tuscan columns) and *Bishop's Castle*.

Bridgnorth (1883): like Ludlow, an excellent Norman hilltop castle planned town, with the same mixture of styles and materials. Start in High Town at C17 island Town Hall (1). Attractively small-scale (2) to site of gate (3). Then former 'Crown' (4) with new loggia, Venetian windows, bow window; (5) as far as timberframe pubs; fine Georgian 5-bay (6) through 1740/1910 gate (7) with loggia; past pedimented almshouses (8) to nice close around church (9)—1889 quadrangle, crude Ionic porch, 6 pilastered gables, pilasters, C18 school.

Good loop from (1). Fine timberframe with figures (10), good shopfront, pilastered corner; excellent frontage with alleys (11)—one with curved gable. Past ornate early-C18 house (12) down picturesque Cartway (13) with sandstone caves to groundfloor weavers' windows (14) and superb 1580 timberframe. Over bridge to bow shopfront (15), pub dummy windows (16), late C17 house (17) with stone surrounds next to scroll doorway; and blank arcade opposite rusticated pilasters (18), out to redbrick corner

(19). Back over bridge to elaborate terrace range (20), up steps (or cliff railway) to good stucco (21), round into fine Georgian street (22), to rectory Venetian windows facing C17 gables and Telford's church portico (23).

Shrewsbury (1884/5): a marvellous town—urban, curving streets, on hill, with probably best timberframe in Britain; delightfully intricate, with many lanes and alleys—explore within river loop in detail.

From castle (1) and C17 school (2) along lanes: (3), to fine gateway and courtyard (4), down to Water Gate (5). Good around St Mary's (6) plus stone portico. Past curious corner top gable (7) to late C17 with segmental doorway (8) and most spectacular carved timberframe, both sides at (9) and (10). Delightful around open Market House (11)—Georgian aprons, timberframe balusters, pedimented Music Hall. Past 8 pilastered windows to churchyard (12) and Georgian/timberframe corner (13)—beginning of fine Georgian quarter. Down past housefronts (14), along Town Walls (15) past RC cathedral to see backs. Then crescent (16) with fan windowtops opposite coupled Doric doorways, stone walltower and stucco chapel (17). Up to (18), gabled 1628 house (19); to Clive house (20), and pediment and pilasters. From (19) along (21) with Venetian doorways to (22)—see backs from park. Along line

of walls: Georgian St Chad's and houses (23), terraces (24)—stucco, recesses, tripartite windows.

Over C18 bridge to extramural Frankwell: nice group (25) with pilasters, timberframe with baluster pattern (26), uphill (27) to Georgian almshouses (cupola) and Darwin birthplace. Back to excellent mixed Mardol—(28), Rowley's house (29), (30). Then delightful alleys (31), (11), (32), (33). Down (34), up to 1700s Guildhall (35), down again to fine frontage (36)—Georgian 'Lion', Gothick glazing, unusual C15 timberframe (with lanes and 1724 school behind); and to Greyfriars houses (37) and fine porch.

Finally across C18 bridge to extramural Abbey Foregate: C14 pulpit (38), group (39) with curved gables, terrace and pilastered pub, between two grand Georgian houses (40) past brick and stucco terraces to 1580s mansion; from (41) early C19 houses (some Gothick), plus timberframe and gaps, right out to stone terrace and huge Doric column.

Much Wenlock: a fine urban village with some stone. From church explore: NE past stone terrace (ogive window) to priory ruins; NW past 1780s almshouses; SE past little terrace (stone back, brick front) and bowfronts out to 'Royal Oak'; and, best, SW down sinuous High Street past loggia, good shopfronts, spectacular 1682 timberframe (balustrades) out to inn with domed bay windows on A458.

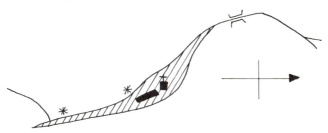

Newport: a good Georgian redbrick town (some stucco, timberframe) with wide cigar-shaped main street and island—SW of which are twirly windowtops, aprons and 1740 rainwaterhead. Explore round island (and church). To S: pilastered windows and strange hood over columns (*), rash of keystones, two timberframe (*), right to recessed double doorways opposite fine chapel. N of church, pilasters everywhere (in pavilions and wings of school, stucco hotel, little terrace), with characteristic curved windowtop/keystones, quoins, segmental windows. Excellent group, gap and canal, then good curving street to junction (fine stucco villa, little pediment on fork).

Ludlow (1884): for many people the perfect historic town, a Norman gridtown with contrast between commercial High Street at top with islands and encroachments, and two fine wide residential basically Georgian streets to s with excellent doorways; many fine Georgian redbrick and painted houses and black and white timberframe. See page 30 for its history. Start at Castle Square (1) with C14 stone/timberframe opposite fine porch. First past 1600s lavish details (2), Georgian mansions (3) to bridge (4). Then wide Mill Street: stucco pediments (5), Guildhall (6) with Gothick details and cupola to medieval school (7). Then into delightful intricate area: early C18 town house (8) with segmental tops; Quality Square; pedimented almshouses (9), delightful 1743 Buttercross. Down through gate (10), fine timberframe (11); timberframe islands and spectacularly carved 'Feathers' (12). N to Corve bridge: nice pairs (13), stone (14) with elaborate 1840s front, and excellent timberframe street—off map.

Finally good loop from (12): blank arcade and timberframe (15), corner of town walls (16), infill housing (17) to medieval chapel arch and bridge (18). Back up (19)—raised pavements, cobbles through gate with Gothic bay window to fine Broad Street: 8 Venetian windows (20); stone pedimented (21); up lanes, terrace (22) and good houses (23); even quoins and urns (24); several pilastered, to timberframe row on loggia (25).

Worcestershire

An attractive rich agricultural county, with many orange/red Georgian houses, often with carved keystones, and exposed black and white timberframe. The abbey town of *Malvern* has a few Georgian and Regency houses, but is basically a Victorian spa. For *Broadway* see page 74. *Upton-on-Severn* is a delightful little town.

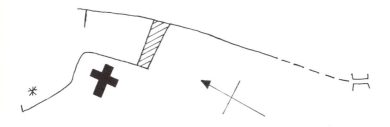

Pershore: a most attractive little town. First from fine abbeychurch NW up medieval timberframe Newlands; behind (*) prize-winning new vernacular housing. Then to Georgian town with coaching inns at Broad Street (market place?), next to 4 Venetian windows plus door, row with 3 pedimented doorways. N up commercialised High Street to grand with clock and stucco opposite tripartite windows.

Finally S to bridge down fine Georgian street with excellent details: bay windows (often 2-storey in pairs), rusticated pilasters, fine doorways and shopfronts (Gothick glazing)— redbrick, and stucco with fine ironwork. W side, stone corner inn with barrels, castellated bay window. Best E: segmental windows, canopies, huge fanlight (lion), to exceptionally grand Perrott House. Best now W side: parapet bullseyes, smaller Perrott with steps and railings, school round openings, warehouse, pair with doubly curved doortops, superb door canopy on fluted columns, bargeboards at edge of town.

Worcester: fine Georgian churches and redbrick houses, and much worth seeking out—despite 1960s *cause célèbre* of new roads and development severing town from cathedral, and, more recently, bad new shops and Inner Ring Road.

SE of cathedral. Nice row and Edgar Street with good details; across canal 1500s Commandery (*), pediment, right, 1740s row.

E and W of High Street. N up best Friar/New Street with excellent timberframe including superb late C15 Greyfriars (courtyard), good shopfronts; at Cornmarket, house (rebuilt) with aprons and rusticated pilasters, foretaste of local Baroque. Then W: good (isolated window pediments) to church (right 1570s house opposite Gothick facade). Down Broad Street: Venetian windows and domed belvedere (*), stucco inns with pilasters, to Georgian terrace approaches and bridge (fine riverside warehouses). Back to top of Broad Street.

Georgian spine (good doorways). N along The Cross—rusticated pilasters and quoins, good group with church (and up alley); then left, Angel Street (Corn Exchange columns) and Shaw Street (double Doric doorways), delightful 1700s hospital (courtyard, chapel), right 1900s terracotta; railway, museum, stone Shire Hall portico, pedimented terrace; right 1873 almshouses, fine Baroque house (school—scalloped aprons, elaborate centre); delightful Regency stucco squares to left (pilasters, balconies and verandahs, shutters—to N one battlemented, one Egyptian) and past terrace to N (house with Moorish tented roof).

s to High Street: E side, inn Ionic pilasters (side roundel), w side, 2 sets of quoins, stucco with pilasters, lavish 1720s Baroque Guildhall. Back past St Nicholas to High Street. Past timberframe to 245 ft spire and chapel (*); back to late C17 corner house near cathedral.

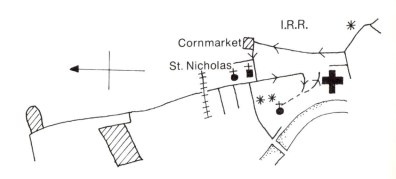

Evesham (1884): an abbey town, pleasantly mixed materials, tree-lined streets. Start at abbey belltower (1); through C12/17 gateway to Market Place (2) with island Town Hall (arcade) and Booth Hall (timberframe). Down nicely dense Bridge Street: left, shallow bow windows, overhanging timberframe; right, parapet with urns, purplebrick with pedimented windowtops, picturesque hotel courtyard (3). Over bridge and up pleasant curve to Venetian windows. Opposite, stone terrace (4) with good shopfronts, mixed group, pair with porch canopies, to pilastered Regency villa (5). Back to delightful churchyard with medieval vicarage (6); pedimented mansion house (7), stucco terrace on waterside (8).

Back over bridge, N to gabled timberframe (9) and delightful brick terrace (10) with Gothick windows. Out to broad High Street with Georgian redbrick and stucco—best house (11) with little pediment in stringcourse, 1692 rainwaterheads and fine ironwork. Then S through alley: superb townscape sequence to (2) and (1). Out to good group (12)—keystones, pilasters, carved eaves; past trees and cobbles to rubble and timberframe abbey remains (13); past timberframe to C17 school (14) and redbrick pair.

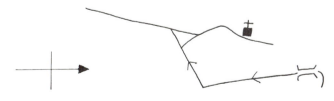

Tenbury Wells: a small, largely early C19 town, plus fiery Victorian brick, with nice plan. Start at bridge, and C17/18 wing of

'Swan': good shopfronts; pilasters of brick and stucco (pub and bank); redbrick pair on left. Along stream, corrugated C19 Gothic pumproom with steeple; turning right, black and white Georgian and timberframe (lozenge pattern on 'Royal Oak'). Explore round oval markethall (Gothick tracery), past rectory with Ionic porch to redbrick row E of church. Return past Georgian pair (Gothick porch shafts) and good stucco house to timberframe and redbrick Cross Street—past C17 round gables to fine Pembroke House.

Bewdley (1883): a delightful Georgian and timberframe river port. From Telford's bridge, first E into Wribbenhall: terrace setback, good timberframe; NE from Jacobean redbrick and pilasters (1), opposite bressumers; turn right at 'Black Boy' to nice redbrick area (2); SW past malthouse row to C17/18 gables (3) and segmental windows (7 painted) along river. Over bridge and SE along Severnside, past elaborate first floor window and shell door to pub with pedimented door and wings (4), timberframe brackets. Inland past terrace (oval), out to edge of town (5)— recessed arches, fine rectory. Into town, left up lane beside almshouses to 1607 school (6); and along attractive High Street: on left, fine Georgian (chapel behind); right, Gothick chapel glazing, to excellent new backland garden (7), 3-storey hotel bows. Beyond corbelled 1610 timberframe (8), left uphill: past almshouses (recessed doorway) to bow window (9); and W to intricate cottage area (10).

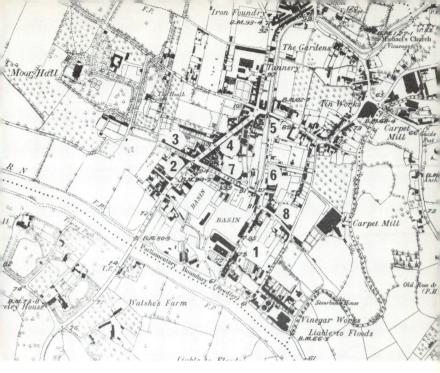

Back to Severnside (11). From bridge superb wide Load
Street: on right, pedimented centre and Venetian windows,
shopfront columns, bows and lettering of 'George', 2-storey
bay/oriels; on left, recessed arch, decorated keystones, Gothick
glazing, to best group—stone Town Hall, timberframe gables,
narrowing at fine Georgian (quoins, keystones); elaborate central
windows under pediment capped by eagle (12).

Stourport (1883): the Georgian redbrick port that replaced
Bewdley, created by canal joining river in 1772. Explore delightful
basins, one now filled in (1); locks; Tontine boatmen's dosshouse
and warehouse with clock. Then to good street frontages (varied
keystones/windowtops): (2), (3), (4) to Tuscan porch of 'Swan'.
Return down towing path (5), past nice warehouses to good row
(6), and streets: (7) with stucco villa and three grandest houses
(quoins, columned doorway with laurels and head, Venetian
doorway); and (8) with good pairs (bow windows, wide
doorways), ironwork, little terrace.

8 Central England

Bedfordshire

Bedford has suffered high growth and much redevelopment, so, like Northampton, has now only small historic areas left.

Woburn: a delightful village—largely of Georgian brick. From cobbles round island Market House: to SE long 'Bedford Arms', quoins and ogive arches (even to Venetian windows), out to house with bow window; to park and church. Best N with excellent shopfronts: on left, twirly windowtops, detached house with 2-storey column entrance and side pediment, old chapel and C16 school, pilasters and bay windows, to gabled 1850s almshouses; on right, 4-storey bows/Venetian windows (Gothick details), keystones, aprons, segmental windows, pilasters, then inn with pilastered bay windows, quoins and combined doorway column/bracket, Gibbs doorway.

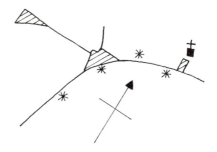

Ampthill: a little town, basically Georgian but with also some timberframe (plastered). At nicely staggered road crossing: Moot Hall cupola, wide Corinthian doorway, twirly windowtops, 'White Hart' pilasters and window surrounds with keystones—next to redbrick house with advanced centre (*). Nice uphill to little green. To S, scrolly doorway and Venetian window, excellent fanlight (*). To N, good new infill shop, following curve of street. Finally fine street E to church: on left, shopfronts with fluted pilasters (overhang), long Georgian house with laurel doorway (*), and C18 gates and piers opposite house with a 3-storey centre on columns (*). Facing churchyard 7-bay house with twirly windowtops, almshouses, another column/hood doorway.

Buckinghamshire

Much timberframe—as likely to be plastered as exposed, and much Georgian brick—often using blues and reds in one house. But at N delightful urban village of *Olney* is built of stone, with many tripartite windows. *High Wycombe* has fine Georgian houses up to its attractive guildhall and Market Hall, with their open ground-floors; four tree-lined redbrick Georgian streets meet at the centre of *Old Beaconsfield*. And *Aylesbury* has an excellent area between its Market Place and church: C14 'King's Head' in lane; good streets to Temple Square, from it s and w, and to church past museum.

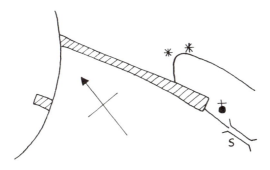

Marlow: mostly built in Georgian brick, often two types in one house. From 1830s suspension bridge good High Street up to obelisk and pilastered 'Crown' (once Town Hall) with varied bow windows; on left mid C19 quoined windows, roundel; on right, Victorian gables (in little green), two pediments, yellowbrick with stone porch, plastered timberframe; up lane to fine Baroque mansion (*), conglomerate medieval/Georgian (*) to pleasant group (one *stone*, curved gable) near river. Up nicely curving West Street: s side, pilastered houses (one rusticated), two pedimented, to grand house with fine stables (cupola); N side row with delightful Gothick windowtops, flint and redbrick school (1624 centre); s side hipped 1690s house with shell doorway.

Amersham: excellent 'Old Town' High Street. Starting at E end, s side: curved window aprons (setback), bow windows, timberframe plus yard. Up street minor terraces to yellowbrick villa. N side, timberframe often behind stucco. Lane past church to weatherboarded stables, Gothick flint cottage, Grecian pilasters and twirly bands opposite brewery arches, good doorways. Back to Island 1680s Town Hall next to cobbles and porch over pavement. s side good group: stucco corner, brick window surrounds and Gothick glazing, 1735 rainwaterhead, to excellent irregular timberframe roofscape; chapel (set back) with female heads on keystones and glazed lantern with urn; grand house with tripartite doorway; C17 almshouses with doorway motif; two huge bay windows; parapet; out to C17 house with room over porch. Returning N side: 1700s crosswindows; cottages becoming houses with good doorways; Grecian 'Red Lion' with pilasters and eaves frieze; C17 gables plus bay windows.

Buckingham (1885): A delightful little town with a complex plan and much redbrick Georgian. In front of 1780s Town Hall (1) classical porch, pilasters both sides, islands with timberframe, fine Georgian house (2), castellated C18/19 old gaol to wide street with trees, good timberframe and Georgian group (3), pilastered chapel (4). Back to bay window and chantry chapel with Norman doorway (5), classical bank. West Street has Georgian houses with fine doorways: in pairs (6); pediment and 9-bay purple/redbrick house with pilasters (7); to stately 1700 Castle House (8) with recessed pedimented centre, stone surrounds, segmental door and window.

Back to (1) and delightful area round church (on site of castle): nice street (9) with C19 pilastered house, curving up to street with C17 house and vicarage, Tudor Manor House (10). Round old churchyard to two good houses (11)—with quoins, stucco with Ionic pilasters. Down to Miller's house (12) with arched doorway and first-floor window; nice lane (13) with a timber anglepost. To fine Castle Street, rebuilt after 1725 fire: grand house with quoins and band (14), door with circular grooves; classical bank type beside huge tripartite windows flanked by pilasters.

Derbyshire

Little now left of historic *Derby* (except Georgian Friargate), but two other excellent contrasting towns either side of the Peak District.

Buxton (1882): built of stone. From Market Place (1) of original market town, over 1000 feet high on hill, with c18 'Eagle', down past good c18 door (2) to the later spacious spa town and Victorian resort in the valley—with cast-iron shopping arcades like Llandudno. It has the spectacular architecture of John Carr's 1780s Crescent (3), c17 Old Hall (4), 'The Square' on arcades, the pavilion/opera complex (5), and the Devonshire Stables, now hospital (6) with a huge cast-iron dome. Fine houses round the gardens—many with classical doorways between double bay windows (7).

Ashbourne (1885): a mixture of stone, brick and stucco. Medieval plan with delightful cobbled pedestrian lanes up to Market Place from main street, and good, largely Georgian, buildings. From early C18 almshouses (1) and fine cruciform church, a superb start: C17 grammar school (2)—symmetrical gables and Renaissance doorways; two houses with similar pedimented centres, grand porches and side windows, Venetian windows, stables with recessed arches—one stone with 3-storey bay windows, one brick with balustrade. Then left, chequerbrick row with big surrounds, Gothick doorshafts; right, C17 almshouses, segmental doorway. Past new road, C19 stone bank with nice frieze (3); on right, triglyph and hood doorways, two huge Ionic pilasters, open courtyard with nice window surrounds (4). Down street to stone bridge; and fine stone bank with recesses, Venetian windows (5). Back and to 'Green Man' (6) with courtyard and sign across road. Then 7-bay house with semi-circular and Venetian windows, to Venetian doorway and Gothick fanlight each side (7).

Back past corner pub with heavy surrounds/keystones (8) up along E side of Market Place: Georgian house with bullseyes; Market Hall; porch on slender columns; brick with 1712 marriage lintel near nice quoined corner (9), good up to church (10). Along upper street past gaps to fine Georgian house (11), cast-iron pump, nice cottages (12), and down steps (13) back to church.

Leicestershire

Leicester, blitzed by Inner Ring Road and bad redevelopment, has only historic areas.

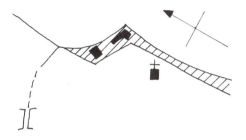

Melton Mowbray: largely Georgian redbrick, with pleasant spaces and street pattern. From stately cruciform church: s to two good stone houses (medieval, 1640s) and Georgian houses out to railway; N to Market Place with projecting 1700s house and 9-bay terrace with pediment. w towards river, C18 redbrick masking C17 stone and good Georgian; and N, pleasant mixed townscape with C19 Corn Exchange.

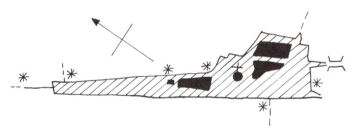

Market Harborough: start from superb C14 steeple: C17 timberframe school/market hall (*) opposite stucco inns (bow/bay windows, C18 sign); nice little stucco/brick street with classical shopfront on corner (*), keystones, quoins. s to Georgian redbrick house (*) with band, and pair of C18 stone houses (*). To N, 1780s Town Hall (pediment, Venetian windows). Beyond, fine wide Georgian street. On left, rebuilt house with pilasters and pediment, Tuscan inn porch, to good redbrick closing street. On right, C17 gabled stone house (*), round windows, stucco with Victorian stone bow windows, whitebrick club, interesting facade with advanced and hipped centre, nice iron balcony, classical chapel (*). Road narrows at row with pendant doorways, house (*) beyond with quoins and porch on slender columns.

Ashby-de-la-Zouch (1886): largely Georgian redbrick. From castle (1) and church, and nearby pedimented school (2) along pleasantly curving street to wide main street: descending with islands, C19 stucco, Georgian brick house with 3-storey bow windows, classical 1840s Market House (3), timberframe. Uphill to fine Georgian house (4) with projecting wings. Then neo-Norman RC church (since map) by Victorian cross (5), into early C19 Grecian spa quarter: a stone terrace (6) has tripartite windows at ends and middle, ironwork, groundfloor pillars; massive hotel (7) with prominent porch (Ivanhoe Baths behind now demolished); excellent classical stone 1849 railway station (8). Return to church past two terraces—one redbrick (9), one rendered (10) with linked round windows.

The new Leicestershire includes the former Rutland, with two delightful little towns.

Uppingham: has excellent stone High Street (C17/18) plus C19 school. In Market Place, curving classical shopfronts, Georgian house with delicate surrounds and fanlight. To E: on left quoins, surrounds with keystones, C17 bay windows and gable; on right 1700s house with 7 segmental windows plus frieze at eaves, bow windows, some stucco and redbrick to C18 gateposts of the Hall (*) with nice courtyard. Nice loop: brick chapel, past the Hall, bow windows with fluted pilasters. Then W. On left, C17 bay windows,

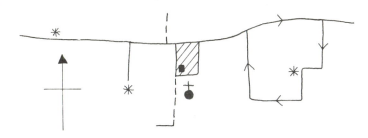

good shopfront, splendid school townscape—fluted pilasters up lane, C18 stone building (*), 1890s block with tower. On right C17 gables, house dated 1787, redbrick, out to nice group including porch on fluted columns (*).

Oakham (1885): an intricate plan and a mixture of materials. Near church C16 school (1) and timber Market Cross (2), near chequerbrick Georgian house with stone quoins. Behind stone Georgian house, superb late Norman castlehall; in front, rest of Market Place with island and good, mixed C17/18 group. From crossroads: stone house with C17 windows/C18 door and nice curving street (3); good C18 houses ahead—stone (surrounds, quoins), museum, with ovals (4); right, stone/brick/thatch street (5). Back along High Street (with several chequerbrick): several stone (sundial) and coupled pilasters of hall, opposite fine medieval house (6)—timber overhang, C14 door, C16 windows. Then redbrick terrace (7) out to 1700s house with doorhood (8). Nice curve (9)—little terrace with keystones, C17 bay windows, C18 stone, to church spire. Opposite, Georgian redbrick house with Gibbs surround windows, doorway with broken pediment (10).

Northamptonshire

Northampton's historic character was eroded in the C19, and high growth and bad development have finished it off in the C20. Now only severed Sheep Street with stone houses up to the Round Church; good sw corner of Market Place with C17/18 pilasters; little Georgian terrace near St Giles; and a splendid group of C17 All Saints and Sessions House and C19 Town Hall.

Oundle (1885): a delightful stone-built town with many C17/18 houses, stone slate roofs and two-storey bay windows. Island Town Hall in Market Place, to N colonnade (1). To S, house (2) with Doric pilasters and balustrade; broad window surrounds and oval; keystones and aprons; 10-bay with rusticated doorway. Past superb 1626 'Talbot' (3) to Victorian school townscape—in courtyard C18 house (4) facing churchyard. Then West Street: left, Georgian shopfronts, detached 1700s house (5) with Baroque twirls under pediment and beside window; simple window surrounds; pilastered gateway; on right, C17 with Gibbs surround; three characteristic bay windows; almshouses (6) with spirelets. Round neo-Byzantine church: classical houses with identical doorways (7); nice cottages downhill (8); C18 with bow windows (9), and gabled dated 1640—and sharp edge of town.

Back to (1), and N towards river. On right up alley good porch (10); two Georgian; gabled 'White Lion'; grand house (11) with centre picked out by quoins; simple Regency by contrast; Jacobean hospital courtyards with doorway on volutes (12). Nice winding street to edge of town; on left, extraordinary curving tops (with keystones) to doors and windows; right, good doorway, classical shopfront, granary with hoist.

Brackley: a little town with a good wide main street of stone, brick, stucco—the two schools giving it a medieval character. Coming up from bridge: on right, good stone group (classical shopfront, keystones, Venetian window under pediment); island 1706 Town Hall with twirl above window. Then on left chequerbrick Georgian, and four pilastered houses—pub (Venetian window, ironwork), brick with bands and keystones, rendered with stone pilasters, elaborate stone with Gibbs surround; cast-iron porch and neo-Jacobean school. On right, Georgian (keystones), Victorian school and C13 chapel, scroll doorway, thatched pub, Georgian stone. Further N is the original village settlement—with church and C17 almshouses.

Nottinghamshire

Nottingham is not covered, being a historic city.

Mansfield: irregular street plan with some chunky C17 stone buildings. Attractive Market Place with classical Town Hall and County Court and fine C18 Moot Hall with colourful coat-of-arms—behind which is pedestrian street with good new Littlewoods and Baroque style pub by medieval cross; follow Church Street under viaduct to late C17 house with segmental doorway, N of church.

Southwell: the Minster was only made a cathedral in 1884, so it has no precinct and is visually part of the small town—with fine detached mostly Georgian houses to its W and N. Pleasantly staggered urban crossing at town centre; follow King Street NE to the green, cross and houses of the Burgage.

Newark (1884): a town of orange/red Georgian brick (plus some timberframe), tatty in places. Surprisingly extensive to E (1); and past house with fine stone doorway (2) into Georgian industrial area near river (3). Start at superb cobbled Market Place, beside magnificent church with 240 ft spire: fine stone 1773 Town Hall; island; early C18 buildings on loggias—the 'Clinton Arms' with Gibbs surrounds and pedimented windows; fine timberframe C14

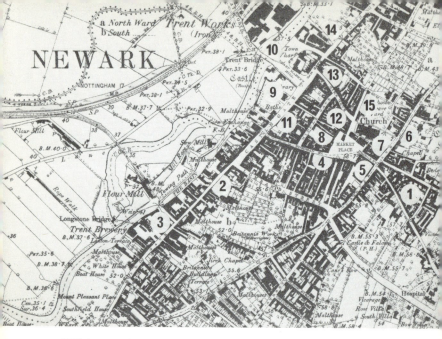

'White Hart' with plaster figures on uprights and C17 overhanging Governor's House (4); behind, good new infill shopping.

3 good loops. First through arcade, good street (5) to two pedimented houses (6) each side of C16 stone Grammar School; back by lane (7). Then by lanes (8) to castle (9) and bridge (10), pedimented houses (11) of Castlegate, back past (4). Finally through Queen's Head Court (12), along Kirkgate (13), to grand house with rusticated doorway (14); returning to see church spire framed between timberframe, and to simple regular 1770s street—half demolished (15).

Staffordshire

Stafford has only a historic area; and *Tamworth*, a redbrick Georgian historic town in the 1950s, has been largely destroyed by recent high growth, leaving only nice streets up from bridge (near castle entrance), right to fine C18 island Town Hall; good houses in Lichfield Street—though one side 'opened out' for tower blocks. *Tutbury* is an urban village with good houses in High Street plus castle and Norman priory church.

Lichfield (1883): a fortified close separated by water from C13 planned town, with some timberframe but mostly grand Georgian redbrick. From cathedral w end, into Vicar's Close (1); then along cathedral approach (steps, pedimented stone) to site of gate (2). Past elegant railings to 1500s hospital (3) with 2-storey porch, opposite Erasmus Darwin's house with Venetian windows. Over bridge to window surrounds of 'Swan' (4) and Baroque window details. Opposite stucco pilastered 'George' up decayed street to good group (5); through garden across new road to C14 Friary remains (6). Then good street (7): left, 1680s house; right, bulgy keystones and centrepiece, stucco (elaborate surrounds) with loggia, little terrace, 1490s chimneys of hospital. Beyond railway bridge Venetian windows (8).

Back down (7) and to fine timberframe (9), pilastered Baroque house (aprons, centrepiece), Guildhall, gables on new loggia. Up curve to little green (10), to medieval cottages amid new housing (11). Above Stowe church two 1750s mansions. Back and into Market Place (12): good statues, careful infill. Ashmole house with Venetian window (13). Past C17 Johnson house to excellent double bowfronts (14). From (12) delightful alley (15); good street to cathedral apse; beyond, fine 1680s stone palace and C18 brick deanery.

Warwickshire

Famous for its exposed black and white timberframe, with a characteristic Georgian redbrick. *Coventry* has fine historic area around cathedral spire; and *Shipston-on-Stour* (good coaching inns, just off A34) is an attractive little town, as is *Henley-in-Arden*, with an excellent long timberframe street (near cross, fine pedimented stone house). *Kenilworth* has an attractive street towards castle, N of Abbey Green.

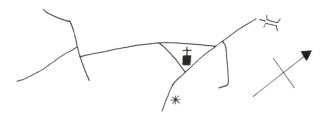

Alcester: delightful timberframe, stucco and brick irregular area round church and island arcaded 1618 Town Hall (near broken pedimented window). Explore streets shown in map: W of church nice lane with battlemented house; SW to recessed Venetian window (*) on Stratford road (some good houses towards roundabout and Worcester), and S past gaps to good group; SE past pilastered Leamington-style house down delightful lane with excellent in-fill housing behind (*); N towards bridge and E up lane to good redbrick chapel (Gothick glazing).

Stratford-upon-Avon (1886): timberframe (most after 1590s fires), but also good Georgian with characteristic chequerbrick. Start at centre of 1196 grid (1)—C18 Town Hall, 1883 terracotta, carved cornerpost. First (2)—elaborately carved brown-and-white, gabled and overhanging both sides, pilasters, round good shopfront curve to Dutch gable (3). Then past timberframe with long burgage plot (4), irregular C15 hallhouse (5) opposite pediment, timberframe strip windows. Over tramway bridge (6) to late C17 (7) and medieval (8) hotels; back over 1480s bridge with Gothick tollhouse (9), to coaching inns—pilasters between gables (10) and cupola (3).

To Shakespeare's birthplace (11) and, behind, to chequerbrick area—between pilastered ranges (12) with Corinthian porches right, Ionic left, to stucco row and chapel (13). Then to triangular marketplace (14), pair with columned windows (15), Wealden-type 1520s timberframe (16); neo-Tudor house (17) and huge pub windowtop, past (1) and (5) to Victorian theatre buildings (18), C17 pilastered gable (19), irregular roofs (20) and church (21). Into

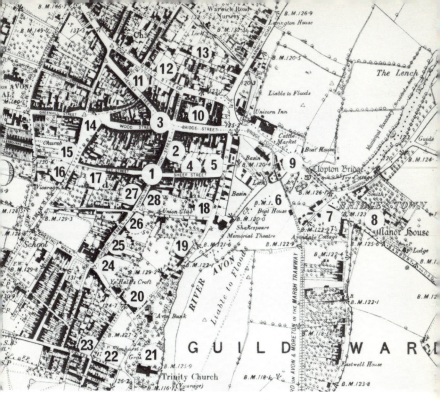

second chequerbrick area, past college remains (22), blank arches (23) to Gothick villa, aprons and good Georgian opposite neo-Tudor curve (24). Finally best streets: pilastered brick and stucco pairs (25); timberframe range with wing windows (26) opposite Gothick front; timberframe hotels, 1673 pilasters (27), Gibbs doorway (28).

Warwick (1887): its centre rebuilt after 1694 fire—so planned and early c18, with best timberframe on fringes, especially on original route (1) over medieval bridge, replaced by new bridge (2) in 1793. So start at unexpected timberframe suburb (3), past carved heads (4), over bridge (2) to superb street (5)—Gibbs doorway, ending with spectacular timberframe and view of castle. Then to Market Place, either side of 1670s Town Hall—arcade and nice 1840s stucco (6) opposite Baroque house; down to extraordinary early c17 (7) with curious bay windows. Past corner carved heads to diminutive house with niche (8), past pilastered corner into superb street: festive Corinthian Shire Hall (9) contrasting with sombre Doric Gaol; pedimented and pilastered window in recess opposite; oval and quoins (10); beyond, 1822 gasworks octagons (11) and Leper Hospital (12).

From splendid church (13) good street—fine Adam-like facade (14), to Baroque crossroads—pilasters, segmental windows, rusticated Court House with niche; and good timberframe and redbrick (15). Good to East Gate—best group (16)—and fine Landor House (17). Loop into timberframe suburb: pair with Venetian windows (18), fine C17 mansion (19), more timberframe (20), Gothick house (21) and church, Georgian houses (22). Finally regular Georgian street plus Egyptian doorway (23) and good early C19 inn facade, to climax of Leycester's Hospital (24). Nice small-scale out to 3-storey timberframe (25). N to some early C19 houses (26 and 27).

Leamington Spa (1887): A Regency New Town with spacious tree-lined streets and avenues—pilastered white stucco buildings, excellent delicate ironwork. Fine villas in two best avenues (1 and 2). Perambulation recommended to more formal architecture. Minor terrace (3) and pediment nicely at angle off centre (4);

delightful residential street (5); good frontage facing gardens with superb sharp corner (6), to main shopping street, The Parade; fine 'Regent Hotel' (7) and proud 1880s Town Hall; terrace with excellent two-storey end porch (8); terrace with riverside colonnade (9) opposite huge Victorian church (10)—tower since map.

Into attractive formal gardens (11), past rotunda (12) to new white flats (13), metropolitan terrace (14), Jacobean villa (15), and delightful circus (16) of Regency semis with verandahs; corner (17) with debased capitals; to fine crescent (18) with pedimented windows, continuous verandah. Past Egyptian columned bay window and door (19), between minor terraces (20)—above fascias; across pilastered Parade (21) to fine terraces facing each other (22). Finally failed crescent with later in-fill (23); square with best ironwork (24); crescent (25) with double two-storey bow windows at back (once front); past linked pairs (26) to terrace (27).

9 Eastern England

Cambridgeshire

First the old Cambridgeshire. *Cambridge* is not covered, being a historic city; *Linton* is an urban village with an excellent winding street.

Ely (1886): an attractive little market town, largely of yellow/greybrick, with superb cathedral plus precinct/close. Start down High Street (1)—monastic buildings, pilasters (one Gothick) and alleys, to Market Place (2)—nastily redeveloped but with fine Georgian houses (3). To good houses (4), Doric Shire Hall portico and classical chapel (5). Then wide street (6): fine Georgian houses, terrace and up lane cottages (7) with keystones (on Venetian and oval windows and doors!); left, timberframe both sides of church, C19 almshouses, pilasters on corner (8). Across green (9) with two fine C18 houses and C17 palace, to Ely Porta (10) and medieval houses (11); downhill past bow and Venetian windows, 1740s school (12) to nice area (13). Back past classical shopfronts (one Ionic) and C16/17 buttressed house (14) to delightful riverside area (15) with converted maltings. Uphill back to (2): C17 house in good group (16), timberframe pub opposite fine porch (17).

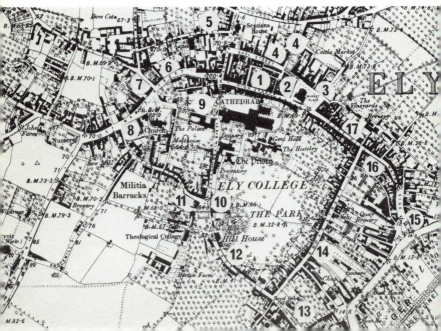

Wisbech (1887): a remarkable Georgian market town/port—
many houses in yellowbrick with redbrick dressings, but decay
and gaps and Inner Ring Road along line of canal. In old Market
Place (1): pedimented double doorway, Venetian and ogive
windows, quoins beside 1840s classical. Across bridge (C17/18
warehouses) into street (2) with pedimented school, little terrace,
house with quoins (setback), Doric doorway, C16–18 school (3).
Then to present Market Place (4)—pilasters of 'Ship', segmental
windows and pedimented inn (5). Beyond church rundown
Georgian area (6). From churchyard into Georgian development
of castle site (7). Greybrick 1840s Museum and Castle Lodge, C17
gatepiers (Regency villa), to yellow/redbrick crescents with two
bands; s side pediment and Baroque window above carriageway, N
infill library; similar street towards (4).

Past chapel with Gibbs surround to C17 gables (8) and famous
houses along river. South Brink: pediment, recessed windows,
stucco for a change, school oval window under pediment with
cupola; to terrace (9) with bow windows at ends, higher parapet in
centre. North Brink: fine doorways, stone bank and Town Hall;
neo-Baroque pilasters and sculpture, stone rustications, three-
storey bow windows (like Weymouth), warehouse, aprons,
segmental windows and Gibbs surround. Then Peckover House
(10)—surrounds with aprons, pilasters, stone doorway, tower
with pilaster, recessed arches; at end splendid 1790s brewery (11).

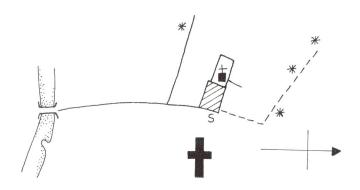

Peterborough: has been blitzed to make it a 'New Town'. Explore from cathedral gateway: ahead to delightful C17 Guildhall; two pubs (C17, C18 keystones); timberframe N of church and grand Georgian yellowbrick with urns and Venetian window W of church. S (classical shopfronts and gabled C17/18 pub) to bridge and C17 Custom House. Best street is Priestgate, W from Town Hall portico: dense in-fill, excellent Georgian, C17 house with plaster overhang and stone mullions, neo-Baroque tower to C18 house, to Doric museum (*) opposite stone house with tripartite windows. N from cathedral gateway, 'Bull' (*) and isolated Georgian stone house (*) and C19 almshouses (*).

Then the old Huntingdonshire.

Huntingdon: basically one long historic street. From medieval bridge (nice warehouses) N: good hotel doorway, past Georgian yellowbrick, good shopfronts to St Mary's with fine house opposite. Then C18 redbrick range (Gothick glazing and door details, pediment, curving windowtops), greybrick terrace and pilastered Institution. New commercial (Co-op has dead 'replica' facade) to excellent Market Place: Town Hall loggia and cupola; C17 house with Ionic pilasters and garlands under windows; Venetian window under pediment; 1727 with delightful pilasters, keystones etc; Norman chapel. Then on left 'George' (C17 timber courtyard), Georgian redbrick, on right sculptural C19 bank, pilasters, Gothick bay window, fluted door columns. Right fork at pretty C18 house with pilasters and railings, out to house with Venetian windows (two at side) and yellowbrick terrace towards station.

Godmanchester: S from medieval bridge. Good stucco houses by sharp edge into good street: several timberframe (Georgian doorways), large C18 (pediment with wings, yellow and redbrick) and minor — to centre by Chinese bridge, good group facing river, right to tiny house with Venetian windows under pediment. The rest is like a village, with some good timberframe houses.

St Neots: superb Georgian Market Place: Doric pillar in centre and pilasters all round (E side in pairs, N side on bay windows). S side: yellowbrick with carriageways, C17 gables, stone surrounds, round and Venetian window under broken pediment, panelled parapet, keystones, parapet and balls (one gone). Good loop: by 1700s house to church; past C18 gates and piers; to Venetian window under pediment in main street.

Kimbolton: fine broad Georgian stucco street from Vanbrugh's great house: left, trelliswork, bow window, good doorways (fanlights); right, ogive window under pediment, rounded shopfront windows, quoins on corner. Delightful East Street: house nicely on corner, C17/18 with plasterwork at eaves and sundial, timberframe.

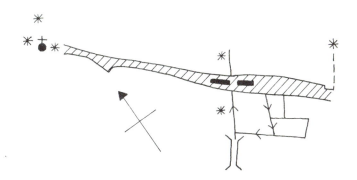

St Ives: a delightful market town. In Market Place: Georgian and neo-Georgian buildings, yellowbrick/stone Town Hall, good pub; N, C19 Cromwell Terrace (*). Follow lane to river, where nice houses and views of pilastered warehouse and medieval bridge (Georgian group far end) with chapel. Inland, two Georgian houses (one pilastered) like pavilions, lower between (*); and C19 classical Institution (*) — like Huntingdon. Towards church: shallow bow window, segmental windows and doorway on brackets; widens to excellent Georgian (Venetian windows). Along river, yellowbrick (rounded windows and doors), with redbrick dressings on corner (*). Facing churchyard C18 bay windows and Gothick doorway (*); to N, good houses — timberframe, another Venetian window (*).

146

Essex

Gets better as one gets further from London, with characteristic weatherboarding, overhanging plastered (sometimes pargetted) timberframe, and Georgian redbrick. The fine urban villages of *Thaxted* and *Dedham*, like those in the Cotswolds, need no more publicity; *Castle Hedingham* has good through road and nice spaces round church; and *Newport* good main street—Georgian pediment, Wealden-type timberframe with recessed centre.

Of the smaller towns, *Great Dunmow* has nice plan. Good stucco doorway next to cross, and to NW, on left, pediment, excellent doorway/fanlight and Georgian black and white inn—facing another in street to N. *Chipping Ongar* has castle site and main street curving nicely down past white ranges (through arch to pedimented chapel) to bridge—from redbrick 'King's Head', columned porch and 1642 timberframe on scrolls. *Wivenhoe* is an attractive little port. From crossroads near church: to W timberframe and pedimented ex-chapel; to N pargetting opposite nice shopfront. To E past elaborate pargetting, and S past Georgian houses to quay—where weatherboarding, redbrick row (nice corner curve), converted granary, pilasters and usual seaside bay and bow windows.

Coggeshall (1881): a delightful little town with much good timberframe and nice plan. From fantastically carved timberframe Paycocke's house (1) and pargetted inn, a good main street (c18 bay windows, two pedimented and rusticated doorways) past 'White Hart' with Georgian middle between gables (2), winding through to 1900s pargetting (3). Explore to nice range (4) by river;

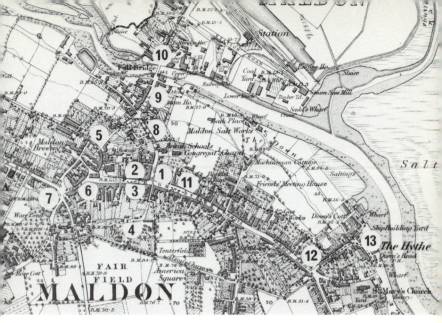

into Market Place (5) past cupola and classical chapel to cottage with 2-storey porch (6). Finally excellent street (7) with pargetting, carved bressumers and good Georgian out to medieval 'Woolpack' (8) and church.

Maldon (1881): an attractive little town on ridge above estuary. From central churchtower/library (1) to C15 redbrick Moot Hall tower plus portico and clock (2) and fine frontage (3)—Georgian red/purplebrick with curly windowtops, $2\frac{1}{2}$-storey with pilasters and frieze across top, pilasters and bow windows, advanced centre with semi-circular and Venetian windows, bow/bay windows and curving porch; behind, across carpark, two fine Georgian houses with columned porches (4). Then triangular churchtower, timberframe row and vicarage in churchyard, stucco street (5)— 'Blue Boar' porch, timberframe behind. On to nice bend (6) with stucco (quoins, 'White Horse' pilastered bay windows, rusticated doorway) and tripartite bay windows and Gibbs surround, gabled and plastered (7), Georgian with shells in window recesses.

Back to (1). Nice curve downhill—stucco bow and bay windows (8) opposite detached house with belvedere and columned porch above classical basement; then stucco and brick Georgian (9) to bridge, good shopfronts (10) and yellowbrick mill plus house. Along ridge from (1) stucco and timberframe gabled houses (11); then commercialised—Victorian bow windows, good pub shopfront, porch on columns (12), down to attractive hythe (13) with Thames sailing barges.

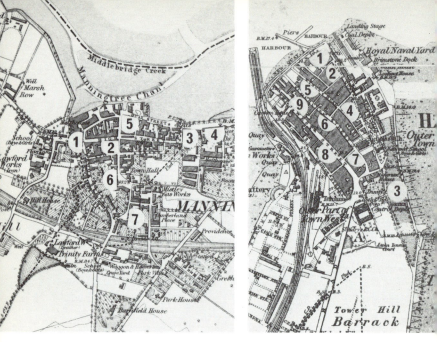

Manningtree (1881): an attractive little Georgian town. From (1) past Ionic porch to pilastered central corner (2); then simple Doric doorways, to good group (3)—one timberframe, and redbrick ranges (4). From (2) to timberframe house and rusticated warehouse (5). Good street uphill to nice group near little green (6), good greybrick houses; to chapel (7) with cupola—influenced by the ruined Adam church at *Mistley*, a mile E, which is a planned Georgian village centred on swan fountain.

Harwich (1881): fascinating Old Town—weatherboarding, timberframe, redbrick Georgian and stucco and new infill housing—the best the latest (6). Explore C13 grid of streets from NE to SW. Start at huge C19 hotel (Town Hall) beside Regency hotel (1) with balcony. Stucco (2), decayed C18 school and Electric Palace, pilasters and seaside bow windows, historic crane (3). Back through churchyard to good group (4); fine mixed frontage (5) with overhanging timberframe, Georgian next to Town Hall. Then two largely Georgian steets—some houses with quoins or advanced centres. In Church Street: first floor window picked out, two houses with apron recesses, good infill (6) to excellent group—1698 in laurel, Guildhall 2-storey bay windows and Gothick/twirly centre, to stucco and timberframe (7). Back along West Street: semi-Venetian window, several pairs—rusticated doorways (8), tripartite windows, ending with two shallow bow windows (9).

Saffron Walden (1881): an excellent little town, of considerable depth, and well cared for. First explore the main spine from cross (1): fine late Georgian with good doorways/porches (one rusticated), Egyptian 1st-floor details (2); to 1832 almshouses and classical chapel (3). Then more commercial and medieval: on left, delicate first floor windows, pedimented Post Office (4); on right, timberframe, recesses, pilasters, corner columns. Then pilasters and nautical bow windows (5) facing timberframe and church spire. Finally delightfully medieval to sharp edge: on left, 1500s courtyard house, and big Georgian (6) up lane, Gibbs surround and timberframe up lane (7); C17 chimneys (8); 'Eight Bells' with C16 windows.

Back to (1) to explore C13 planned town to E. First largely timberframe street — views of church, plaster frieze with dolphins, Georgian complex with archway (9). Through attractive lanes N of (10) to good shopfronts and timberframe (11), and Market Place with C19 refronting to C18 Town Hall and 1840s Corn Exchange. Past C17 brackets on corner (12) to incredible C14/15 timberframe (13) with elaborate carving and C17 pargetted figures, and nice Georgian and cottages (14). Back to timberframe plus charming C19 and bow windows (15), through (16) to long irregular brick and plaster street (17) — two houses pilastered, and past castle mound (18) to The Common, C16/17 Priory (19) with Venetian window, Tuscan school columns (20), early Victorian houses near maze (21).

Colchester (1881): 'More impressive than any other town in England for the continuity of its architectural interest' (Pevsner)—before extensive new development and Inner Ring Road (1), partly along Roman walls (2).

Main spine along ridge to E. Doric columns over pavement (3), pilastered bow windows (4), superb 1900s Baroque Town Hall (5), C15 'Red Lion' (6) with traceried panels, 'George' (7) with ironwork. S to Georgian (8) with oval and pilasters, past house with Gothick details (9) to Norman priory ruins (10), stretch of walls (11). Then fine Georgian brick—Venetian windows and pilasters (museum), gables with oval and oriel (12), pilasters; bay window on columns with folly at back (13). Then gaps and Doric porch (14) opposite twirly windowtops. Off map, beyond brewery on N side, recessed doorway with Empire capitals—opposite pilastered bay window, then minor Georgian and timberframe to green and house with bow windows, bridge; beyond mill good timberframe street (one dated 1692) plus Venetian window over Gibbs doorway, to splendidly irregular 'Rose and Crown'.

N and S of spine. From (3) to largely Georgian street: W side Venetian window under pediment, Gothick door columns (15),

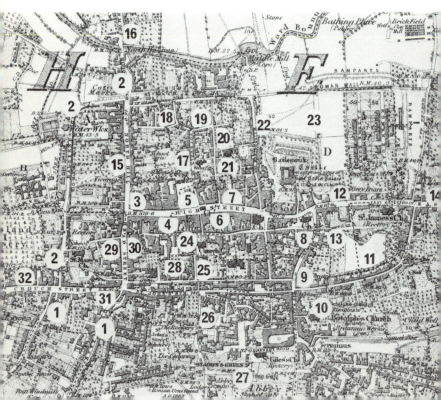

bay windows; E side bow windows, balconies and garlands on keystones, Venetian window. Some timberframe, as beyond (2) over bridge (16). Back to (5) and into delightful 'Dutch quarter': fine timberframe groups, Gibbs doorway (17), two pilastered pairs (Venetian window); at bottom to timberframe (18) and good new housing (19); up past timberframe/Georgian (20), across (21), nice winding timberframe down (22), up through castle park (23).

Finally from (5) to good shopping precinct and Georgian house (24) with gatepiers and archway, and timberframe street (25) down through arch; a yellowbrick terrace (26) leads under ring road to green with abbey gateway (27). Back to (25). Past delightful Regency capped bow/porch (28), to street with bow windows (29) and advanced centre (30), curious doorway and window. Down to street with grand Georgian (31), Regency (32) bow windows, laurels over windows, pilasters.

Witham: nice houses in original village settlement by church. Fine houses along main road through 'new town'. From E: tripartite windows. 8-bay house with shell doorway, grand with good doorway, pilasters and two little terraces—opposite Georgian with elaborate first floor window between two timberframe. Then narrowing, and beyond bow and bay windows of 'Spread Eagle', widens again with good Georgian purple/red or redbrick and central arched windows with keystones; on right, advanced centre, gap, pilasters and aprons and twirly window-tops; on left, advanced centre, bow window, fine pair, 2-storey bay windows and fine fanlight.

Hertfordshire

Surprisingly East Anglian, with weatherboarding and plastered timberframe, sometimes pargetted. *Bishops Stortford* has nice stucco island Market Hall, fine coaching inns, attractive street—like village green—w of church. Despite proximity of London, Herts has some good historic towns, as well as the attractive urban village of *Ashwell*.

Baldock: founded (the name derived from Baghdad) when mid C14 Templars diverted pre-Roman Icknield Way to the present delightful staggered crossing with islands. Four largely Georgian streets. NW recessed pub arches, redbrick row, stucco, C17 shell doorway to timberframe 'Bull'. NE: left, pilastered with advanced centre, 5-bay; right, chequerbrick, pilasters, redbrick; at crossing irregular timberframe with 2-storey porch. SE broad, tree-lined:

right, chequerbrick ending with bay window over porch (aprons, twirly windowtop), Gothick windowhoods, C17 almshouses with Victorian bargeboards; left, timberframe, redbrick, three stately houses (pilasters, pedimented centre, semi-circular and Venetian windows) to nice redbrick/stucco group (keystones). Finally SW and on left best frontage: overhanging timberframe, advanced centre, segmental doorway (good fanlight), quoined yellowbrick with wings — opposite redbrick house with band and quoins.

Ware (1884): many timberframe and Georgian houses, plus good plan with islands in High Street and long burgage plots down to river (C18 gazebos). From bridge: Georgian redbrick above hideous fascia (1); Gibbs doorway (2); pilasters; behind island, chequerbrick (3) with twirly windowtop, archway with niche to Bluecoat Yard (4) with 1690s range and C15–17 manorhouse; yellowbrick Town Hall on arcade; chequerbrick beside stucco with good porch (5); along burgage plots carriageways — explore under 3 gables (6). Up tree-lined walk (7) to good 1860s and 1970s corners and cottage row with pargetting (8). Back to groundfloor Ionic columns (9); C17–18 Priory (10); segmental windows, and 'Bulls Head' oriel and bay windows (11); past roundabout to Jacobean/Gothick house (12). Finally across bridge to timberframe (13); and Georgian with 2 Venetian windows each wing (14), stucco, pilasters (15).

Hertford (1884): many fine Georgian and timberframe houses; complex plan (a Saxon burh each side of river?) plus Inner Ring Road (9). Superb townscape round bowfronted Shire Hall (1): little square—Ionic timber columns; 1700s with scroll doorway (2), good stucco to c16–18 house (3) with gatepiers and urns, gabled to riverhead—with conical maltings. Past 1670s Meeting House (4) to fine Georgian group (5): pediment, pilasters, bay window on columns plus wings, terrace with Bluecoat girls in niches. Back down nice curving street: redbrick opposite columned porch; through arch, 1801 with sundial; stone Corn Exchange (6); good frontage with Victorian stone banks, Georgian 6-bay, pilasters, advanced centre to Egyptian front and shopwindow (7). Past timberframe overhang to superb pilastered Bayley Hall (8)—with *two* fine doorways and Inner Ring Road (9).

Past new civic centre (10), over bridge to Old Cross area (11) with timberframe near river. Round to c19 pilasters opposite Albert dwellings (12); brewery, pediment (13). Back to excellent timberframe/Georgian street: terrace with recessed centre (14); two pilastered houses—rustications, attic storey; to good group (15)—quoins, Gothick details. By path (16), past castle, Gothick cottages (17), underpass (18) to West Street: aprons and converted maltings (19); yellowbrick terraces; doorways rusticated, scroll, 3 shell; to c17 blank arches opposite Gothick glazing (20). Then Castle Street (18)—yellowbrick, timberframe, little pediments; to good final stretch: castellated 1840s (21); Georgian redbrick opposite Gothick glazing, quoins; pilasters (22). Island removed since map. Good final frontage back to (1): rustications and quoined centre, bow windows, and superb pargetting both sides.

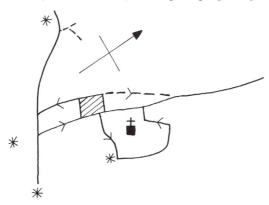

Hitchin: three sallies from Market Place (quoins next to Corn Exchange cupola). First loop E: new arcade, stall canopies, C17 almshouses (*), 1929 pool and terrace; round church to little Georgian terrace (keystones), nice lane and C15 timberframe. From market place N, beside corner Georgian redbrick: commercialised—bow window, 3 Venetian opposite 2 semi-circular windows. To good curving timberframe and Georgian street (advanced centres, elaborate neo-Baroque porch) to C17 almshouses.

Then S—quoins between good timberframe inns with yards opposite good 1840s yellowbrick. Right into attractive street: good gabled overhanging timberframe, stucco (laurel doorway, ironwork), Georgian redbrick (twirly aprons), several rows (band, sets of doorways), to detached Georgian house and excellent 1844 chapel (*). Back downhill past pargetting to conglomerate Priory (*)—cloisters, arcade, garden front with Venetian windows; and similar street (timberframe nicely converted, painted dragons) to stucco inn (*). Finally N up excellent Sun Street: Georgian redbrick; stucco porch and wreaths at eaves opposite ogive doorway and window, bay and round windows; pedimented centre with oval; good shopfront with sign, twirly windowtop opposite 9-bay 'Sun' with segmental windows, assembly rooms with Venetian window in yard.

St Albans (1884): delightful triangular market place laid out in 948 at gate of great abbey (whose immensely long abbeychurch is now cathedral): clocktower (1); overhanging timberframe; chequerbrick (2) facing Town Hall with portico, pilasters, wreaths on windows. Largely Georgian to N and S. N broad and tree-lined: 7-bay house (3) with central surround, then commercialised; (4) to new Civic Square and medieval barns (restaurant); bay and Venetian windows (5); mixed frontage (6)—segmental windows, Gothick glazing; to 1736 pedimented almshouses (7); nice group (8) with ovals; Grecian (9) with curious capitals, 1820s neo-Tudor, grand pilastered with keystones, almshouses (10).

Then S from pilasters and Venetian windows each side (11): C15 'White Hart' opposite chequerbrick; Venetian windows (12), pedimented yellowbrick; Gothick glazing and timberframe (13) with slim porch columns; overhanging corner (14) and up nice mixed street to little terrace (15); good view (16) uphill.

Finally long historic street to St Michael's: ziggurat infill (17); exposed timberframe; Georgian curve (18) to Abbey Gateway— and medieval 'Fighting Cocks' (19). Into early C19 area: pedimented chapel (20), terrace (21), to stucco villas (22). Mansion with pedimented centre (23). Then winding Georgian and timberframe to late C17 opposite Venetian windows (24); 1700s brick windowbands (25); mill (26) plus manor; off map (27) to pilastered stucco facing grand chequerbrick, near church.

Lincolnshire

A large remote county, unspoilt (except on Humberside). *Lincoln* is not covered, but see page 14. *Sleaford* and *Grantham* have attractive areas round their market places.

Louth (1889): a delightful little town with an intricate plan, Georgian/early Victorian purple/redbrick (many tripartite windows). Start from superb 295 ft church spire (1). Pilastered house with recess opposite terrace (2) with pedimented centre and triglyph doorways, to bridge and 1755 mill (3). Then fine Georgian street (4) lined up with spire: s side, advanced centre, 3-bay plus wings (recesses); 2-storey bow windows on columns — opposite gatepiers; pedimented, arched between 3-storey bow windows; to grand 7-bay (5) with segmental windows and pediment.

Then from (1) into commercial centre: past stucco to parabola double doorway (6), past corner pediment (7) and chapel with swags to palazzo-style 1854 Town Hall, on to good houses, doorways and porches (8). Back to attractive central Cornmarket (9) and Market Place — stucco, pilasters, bow windows. Past 3-storey corner bow/bay windows to coupled pilasters (10). Past 11-bay row to overhanging timberframe (11) and excellent group (12) — pilastered stucco (library, good interior), bow windows, Venetian and round windows (curious glazing).

Stamford (1886): delightful street pattern incorporating line of defences of Danish burh and medieval walls (see page 27). Overwhelming in the quality and extent of its stone houses (plus some timberframe)—C17 with multi-storey bay/oriels (often gabled), C18 with big surrounds (keystones or Gibbs), to simpler earlier C19 and good shopfronts (bow windows), plus Colly Weston stone tiles and some Mansard roofs.

Former Great North Road from NW to nice sharp edge at S. C19 almshouses (1); good round All Saints (2)—cobbles, 3-storey bow windows, rusticated pilastered plus cupola (3); nice stretch (4) with buttress, columned corners; delightful cobbled area (two pilastered houses) round St Mary's (5); rusticated Town Hall and 9-bay (6) with advanced centres, opposite Norman doorway; bridge—C17 warehouses and almshouses (7); then uphill conglomerate 'George' (8), Victorian gables, painted timberframe gable (9) and balcony on column; quoins with pilasters and carved eaves; four 3-storey bay windows (10) plus hood door.

Sallies off. SW: Egyptian with splayed doorway (11) by nice churchyard; loop to good crossing (12), down to mill, Gothick bathhouse (13), castle corner; then good street (14) off map to 34-

bay terrace (pilasters and ironwork) and wall tower to N. NW: delightful street (15) to grand early C19 (garlands, balustrades). NE to Broad Street (16) with medieval hospital, to redbrick chapel (17). E down High Street—redbrick, lunette, terrace with surrounds/bands, fluted pilasters (18) to good street, library pediment (19), to school, medieval arch (20), Whitefriars' Gate (21). Finest E past giant columns (5), old theatre (22), nice street off (23), to delightful St George's area and grand 1670s house (24) with rusticated chimney and double dormers; good streets N and E (25–26). Finally over bridge, along river to 1793 maltings (27). Out of town, Norman priory (28).

Boston (1889): with famous huge church and tower, characteristic purplebrick Georgian with tall thin doorways (often pedimented)—tatty in places with new Inner Ring Road (9), but a lively market town and attractive along river and Maud Foster's Drain. 5 sallies from Market Place (1) with stucco pilastered Assembly Rooms—porch on columns with room above, and 15-bay Exchange buildings with recesses, both with pedimented centres and facades to river. First through alleys with timberframe to the 'Stump', C17 gable and riot of brickwork (2), Georgian Wormgate with bowfronts, nice street off (3), 'Barge' (4) with wide doors and windows, to fine houses (5)—ironwork. Then from (1) NE into Wide Bargate: stucco, ironwork, nice streets off (6); good houses (7)—recessed windowtops, 18-bay terrace (8); IRR (9); to windmill (10) and attractive houses facing Drain (11, 12).

Then from (1) S across bridge to pilastered 'White Hart' (13), nice alleys and triangle of streets with 10-bay row (14), and High Street: good warehouse (15) opposite Gothick doorway; new bridge (9); stucco, yellowbrick Gothick chapel (16), round arches, tripartite doorway; pedimented centre (17) with cartouche and garlands between wings with bay windows; and redtiled terrace (18) with strange pilasters/giant arches.

Then from (1) E down Dolphin Lane to little square, Egyptian 1860s Freemasons' Hall (19) and C15 Pescod House (20). Finally to S. Elaborate timberframe (mostly 1874) and C18 Custom House (21). E up lanes: Georgian warehouses, medieval Blackfriars, cobbled cul-de-sac, and good chapel (9). Back to medieval brick Guildhall beside fine Baroque house (22) with pilasters, balustrade, twirly doortop, railings and gatepiers—opposite impressive C17/18 gabled warehouses. To good porch, quoins; across IRR; pedimented house (23), 1576 school (24) in courtyard, nice yellowbrick terrace (25) and medieval Hussey tower (26).

Spalding: basically Georgian brick, famous for houses along river. Start at Town Bridge. First NW to Market Place with two good inns, Prior's Oven (*)—octagonal vaulted shop, through wide New Road and left to pilastered brick school facing Venetian window; back via grand Manor House (*). Then E to church— thatched 'White Horse', yellowbrick pair, neo-Tudor almshouses, good to corner.

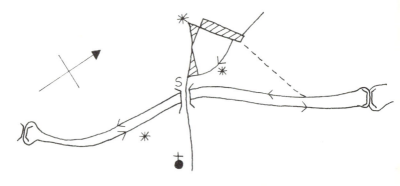

River banks. First to N. E side keystones, balls, rusticated mill, stone surrounds, 2-storey bay windows flanking elaborate fenestration, nice warehouse, Egyptian porch to pilasters and little terrace; cross by footbridge to stone door surrounds, rusticated house and warehouse, pilastered pair and C17 mullioned; back S tatty, with minor Georgian, warehouses, to grand house with wings, purplebrick with quoins, chunky new centre. Then along river to S. W side: pub tripartite windows with frieze; three terraces —6 + 12-bay, 5 × 3 and 9 × 3 (two doorway types) plus 6-bay with porch (lionheads); group with pedimented centre behind gatepiers plus urns, side curving porch, Hall (stepped window-tops, lavish porch). Cross concrete footbridge and back to N: pilastered bow and Gibbs windows; castellated Tower House plus row with keystones; bay windows and balustrade; recessed arches and complex C15–19 Ayscoughfee Hall(*).

Norfolk

An enormous remote county, with characteristic Georgian redbrick, plastered timberframe and flintwork, with almost every town worth exploring. *Norwich* is not covered being a historic city. At the other extreme are the urban villages of *New Buckenham* (grid plan, C17 Market House) and *Burnham Market* (good houses in grassy broad street), and a number of delightful little towns, such as *Wells*, with an attractive staithe, a good street (and lanes) inland to church, and fine houses round the green. The others all have intricate plans and attractive market places with islands: *Holt* with many quoins and rusticated pilasters; *Aylsham* with many pilastered houses, three in Market Place; *North Walsham* with an octagonal timber Market Cross, and *Swaffham* with a similar one in its spacious triangular Market Place lined by fine houses. *East Dereham* has another good Market Place (7-bay house with ovals and double porch, explore round islands, N side bow windows and columned shopfront)—as has *Reepham* (7-bay with elaborate porch).

Thetford (1883/4): despite modern expansion, Thetford's greatest days are past (as can be seen from map), having in C14 20 parish churches and 4 monastic houses plus Blackfriars. Characterised by much flintwork. From bridge (1): S to nice Georgian (2) and flint/brick (3). N, on left good house plus warehouse, pedimented centre, fine timberframe—museum (4); on right, bow windows, good shopfront, C17 gabled wings with Gothick doorway (5). Past timberframe 'Bell' (6) and grand yellow/redbrick house (7) with curved parapet, up pedestrian street to crossing near Market Place (8), and up yellowbrick/flint street to nice group with pilasters (9). Back to Market Place (good corners). Loop, Guildhall Venetian windows, minor Georgian to more good corners (10). Then splendid warehouses plus house, old gaol, bow window to 1694 'Dolphin' and timberframe (11); to return down tree-lined Castle Street past pilastered house (12) and good flint row with brick window quoins (13) back to (8).

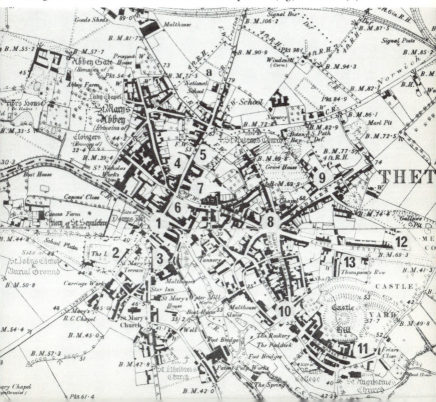

Wymondham (1887): largely timberframe, with several shaped gables. Good houses round fine octagonal Market Cross (1), and up street to c18 gaol (2). To w segmental windows of 'Kings Head' and bressumers (3); nice small-scale street (4) to bridge. Finally good loop. From flint chapel, now library (5) past grandest Georgian house (tripartite doorway, pilasters, pediment), strange rusticated doorway plus sidewindows, pair opposite timberframe with pilasters (6), fork (c17 shaped gable), out to Venetian window opposite exposed timberframe (7). Back past house with arched windows and Gothick glazing (8) to magnificent abbey church (9); return along nice curve past timberframe 'Green Dragon' (10) with original shop windows.

King's Lynn (1886): a major historic town, with warehouses ranging right back to river. Best explored up streets N and s of cathedral-like West Front of St Margaret's—next to Saturday Market Place (1) with c17 pilasters and panel, rusticated gaol, and flint/stone chequer guild and town halls. To N, college gables and medieval doorway (2), greybrick Georgian, barleysugar columns (3) with c16 brick tower behind; left to Charles I under twirl (4) and terrace facing superb 1680s Customs House (5). Then many materials and dates (medieval brick, pilasters, hooded window-tops and scrolls) to spacious Tuesday Market Place—with Corn Exchange, 1680s curved broken pediment (6), a pillared ground floor. Past segmental doorways (7) and timberframe to huge St Nicholas's, grand house with Venetian windows, stucco gables, and terrace on line of walls (8). s of (6), pedestrian High Street (9).

Now s of (1). Past pedimented stucco house to medieval priory and warehouse ranges and c15 Hampton Court. Fine curving Nelson Street with traceried door and pilasters, Georgian red/yellowbrick with huge doorway (10) opposite terrace (recesses), elaborate doorway. Then splendid timberframe fisheries building (11), stucco, c14 gateway (12); through rundown Georgian area with medieval hallhouse (13), to magnificent 1520s South Gate (14). Return past terraces (15) with pediment and honeysuckle bands, and some purple/redbrick houses (16). Into gardens to town wall (17), octagonal chapel (18) and pilastered terrace (19). Back past Greyfriars tower (20).

Great Yarmouth (1885/6): patchy, but much more to explore than CBA's 'market place and remaining rows', including almost complete medieval walls (facing river on W). Unique historic plan, with three N–S streets connected by 150 narrow rows (most destroyed in 2nd World War). Start at the bridge (1). N: bow window and Gothick shopfront (2), pillared shopfront, to Georgian redbrick Broad Row (3). Then fine houses along the Quay: Georgian red and greybrick (bay window, ironwork, quoins), including Elizabethan museum interior (4); Greyfriars ruins (5); Doric colonnade, 3-storey bow window, segmental narrow windows (Customs House), pair with recessed centre, C17 Merchant's House (6) and C14 Tollhouse at back. S to pick up good stretch of town walls (7)—and follow it round to church. To S, 1810 arcaded courtyard (8), and Nelson column (off map). To E 1840s seaside resort development with Wellington Arch (9).

Continuing back N: C17 'White Lion' (10) and Georgian street, one house (11) having curved windows over rusticated doorway; bay and bow windows, reflecting curves of Baroque St George's (12) with walls behind (13). Then commercial street (14) with new shops—incorporating arched stretch of walls (15), to Market Place (16): 1700s Fisherman's Hospital (17), timberframe house, vicarage with shell door. Georgian houses (18) facing huge St Nicholas, and past pair (19), to another stretch of walls (20) and round tower by river (21).

Suffolk

Ipswich is not covered, being a historic city. At the other extreme are four delightful urban villages, Lavenham, Clare, Long Melford and Nayland.

Clare: nice street pattern and 3 houses with clustered Tudor chimneys. W of church, oriel brackets on 'Sun' and vicarage; to S, elaborate pargetting, to N, five gables with Gothick glazing. Nice Market Place, cross and 'Bell'; and beyond good corner, shopfront and wide street to SW: C19 pilasters and excellent timberframe opposite grand Georgian houses (redbrick pilastered and pedimented, symmetrical with wings and patterned chimneys).

Long Melford: walk from rebuilt house with chapel windows S end: Venetian window and some good yellowbrick—left, 1610 figure porch, right, timberframe 'Bull'. Then C16 Hall, green (Tudor star chimney among houses on left), surprisingly urban terrace, almshouses with cupola and church.

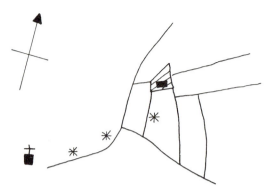

Lavenham: Overwhelming in the quality and extent of its timberframe buildings, with carved overhanging brackets, gable ends, bressumers etc. Starting from church, explore streets shown, the best being: first stretch; right; and left and then right up to Market Place and Guildhall. Note 3 similar grand Georgian houses (*)—two-storey bay windows (columns and pilasters on corners), pilastered with Venetian windows; and contrast between timberframe being exposed (unfortunately increasingly) and traditional plastered elsewhere.

Nayland: good houses round little square and church; and delightful along stream, and over bridge to nice rounded corner and house with 1690 pargetting.

Sudbury: round St Peter's: Town Hall with pilasters and portico, greybrick house with recessed centre; in front, wide Market Hill with good s frontage (first-floor pilastered window, Georgian bay window on columns, Corn Exchange converted into library, Egyptian columns)—from which good loop to sw. Right to Gainsborough house, winding nicely with minor Georgian and timberframe, then good yellowbrick plus timberframe, culminating in spectacular Chantry (carved angel on corner) and Salter's Hall (man and animals on oriel, pebbledash Gothick on side). Pilastered mill (hotel), Cross Street with timberframe opposite Georgian, to good group over bridge. Back past All Saints— timberframe dated 1673 and with bits of priory—where becomes

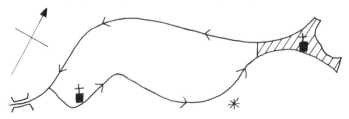

good and increasingly stucco street: N side, doorway with urns and terrace with recesses; S side, pilasters, and grand Georgian house down lane (*).

Woodbridge (1884/7): a delightful little market town. Start at Market Hill (1) with gabled timberframe and Georgian (Egyptian doorway) round Shire Hall. Nice street (2)—'King's Head' oriel on heads, pilastered range with recesses, quoins, pargetted oval wreath. Out to fine timberframe (3) with carved windowheads, back past 'Angel' (4) with bressumers, left down to Georgian recessed tripartite windows (5). Back to (1) and street with slim pilastered doorway, timberframe 'Bell' (6) with hoist for weighing waggons, timberframe window arches. Down nice curve (7) to early Victorian greybrick area: up to and around church (8), urban with pilastered centre (9); out to Regency rusticated and redbrick pair (10).

Back along the Thoroughfare: excellent Georgian group (11)— with wings and ironwork, recesses, advanced centre; amid shops, Regency balconies, 1650s carved wooden frieze, Barry-like stucco (12) and Venetian window. Right, up good street (13) to house (14) with 3-storey C16 porch at back, Georgian frontage (15) and church. Back down to nice houses on former quay (16), and tidemill (17). Finally largely Georgian Cumberland Street: fine doorways—segmental, scrolls, head, and Venetian window (18); timberframe, pilasters; 1670s (19) with hipped roof and semi-Venetian Ipswich-style dormers, out to pediment and good greybrick house (20).

Bury St Edmunds (1884): Norman gridtown laid out by
Benedictine abbey, with a wealth of medieval, c17 and particularly
Georgian buildings—the 'typical' doorway being recessed with
twin columns. Start from Angel Hill—pedimented hotel, stucco
Athenaeum, c14 Great Gate (1). Good yellowbrick round corner
(2) and up street (3)—pilasters, recessed centre between quoined
wings, loggia (4), to edge of map. Along abbeywall good
timberframe (5) with corner post tracery, Abbot's bridge (6), and
house with buttress posts (7). Then two main grid streets: from
Ionic shopfront (8) past two more Georgian shopfronts to market
place encroachments and 1690s cupola house (9). Past medieval
battlemented Guildhall (10) opposite elaborate symmetrical
composition; turn left to good group (11) near Norman belltower.

Into precinct to c18 asylum range (12), pilastered house (13),
pedimented Manor House (14). Back to little square (11) with
ironwork and obelisk, nice street (15)—twin doorways under
pediment, Gibbs doorway; past stone house (16) to delightful
square (17) and to good houses—off map (18). Then past Regency
theatre (19) to best cross streets: (20) with almshouses and (21)—
pair with Venetian window and wings; returning past terraces (22)
and pargetted timberframe (23). Good group (24) near RC church.
Finally excellent Guildhall Street, past (10) to splendid classical
Corn Exchange (25), Library, 1780s Town Hall facing Norman
Moyse's Hall (26).

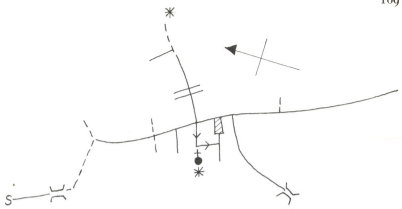

Hadleigh: excellent mixed Georgian and timberframe (much painted white). N end good group N of bridge, then High Street S from fork. W side, redbrick terrace with advanced bays, plain and coloured pargetting (dated 1618), formal Queen Street; E side, Ionic porch, Gothick central window, classical shopfronts, 6 Venetian windows. Left up George Street: nice mixed; new road; on left ogive window, pilasters; on right, chapel recessed arches, pargetting, grand Georgian with fine porch, past gap to Elizabethan with gables (*). Right, up fine greybrick Church Street (Venetian doorway, C17 chimneys) to churchyard with C15 brick gatehouse (*) and timberframe Guildhall—to Venetian and round windows at back, Tuscan portico and delightful Market Place, with nice stucco pair (central window surround), large pedimented house.

Continuing High Street S from George Street: on left, coloured pargetting, bow window and Tuscan colonnade; right, good greybrick and pleasant Duke Street to medieval bridge. Good (white gables and redbrick) for some distance: E side, Gothick doorway; W side, tripartite windows, triglyph porch, Gothick Venetian window, lavish C17 timberframe with brackets, almshouses.

There are three delightful largely Georgian little towns in NE.

Bungay: redbrick, with attractively intricate plan. From L-shaped Market Place (pilasters and bow window, open C17 Butter Cross with statue), sally up streets in 5 directions: Earsham (W between two good inns to bridge), Broad (NW), Bridge (NE to river), Trinity (SE, past churches, to 1700s pilastered house on corner). Finally St Mary's Street: S past grand pedimented house, medieval oriels on carved cills, right at fork to gatepiers and Hall with Venetian window.

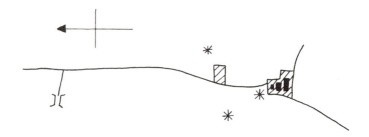

Beccles: many houses with shaped Dutch gables and/or pilasters—often rusticated, as on 'King's Head' in Market Place with islands and dominated by belltower (*). Best streets above river: to S, Ballygate past grand rectory to flint Gothick facade of Leman school; to N, Saltgate to Old Market Place—with two pediments facing each other, behind one fine flint and brick hotel (*), behind the other gabled Ravensmere (*). Then long Northgate with 'scores' down to river, many gables, grand houses, to bridge and maltings converted into flats.

Southwold: a small-scale seaside town with irregular greens and many excellent houses, often pilastered—as in High Street (with also two Gibbs doorways, Dutch gable) from C17 Sutherland House to pump, ironwork and bay windows of 'Swan' in Market Place. From here sally: N up Church Street (row with wide segmental windows facing pedimented twin doorway) and left to magnificent church, right to green, 'Sole Bay' inn and delightful area near white lighthouse; E, nice street to sea and one formal terrace—3-bay yellowbrick each side of 5-bay stucco with shells; and S to spacious South Green with grand early C19 houses (bow windows) and two good streets off to W.

10 Northern England

Cumbria

A rural, largely mountainous county made out of the former Cumberland, Westmorland and part of Lancashire. It has many Scottish characteristics, such as stone, initialled marriage lintels, 'harled' houses with stone surrounds.

At extreme sw, *Barrow-in-Furness* is a late Victorian planned town with grid plan, spacious tree-lined streets and grand public buildings (Gothic Town Hall)—in contrast to *Whitehaven* 30 miles N, another planned grid seaport, equally remote but laid out in 1680s. *Workington*, N again, also has a grid and C18 Portland Square, as has better *Maryport*, laid out 1748–9.

Cockermouth (1867): a most attractive little town. Good townscape E from black-and-white 'Trout' opposite pilastered neo-Grecian villa (1): past grand Wordsworth house (2) (no pauper poet here), two pubs with curious curved door pediments (3), elegant Court House with little clocktower (4), past Venetian doorway (5) to castle (6). Back down to pillared porch (7), up to delightful cobbled street (8) with trees: another curious pedimented doorway plus more standard Georgian. Return across stream via more good houses (9).

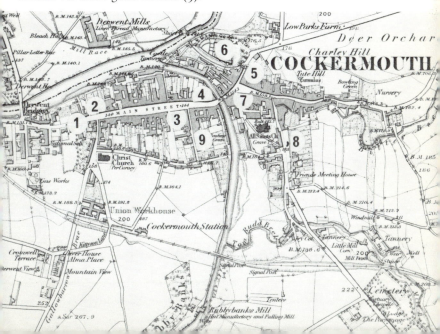

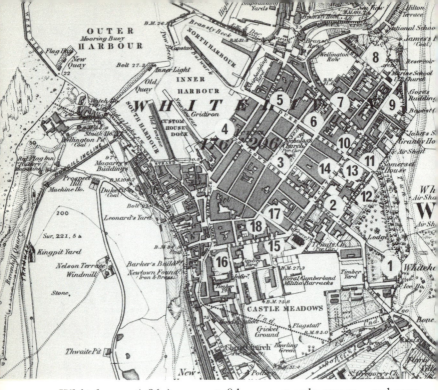

Whitehaven (1867): many c18 houses, mostly stucco—and gaps
and decay. From former Lowther house (1) take main street past
Georgian row (2), block left vacant for church (3), good c19
classical banks to two terraces near harbour (4). Return by (5) to
corner (6); up over good George Street (7) to fine Georgian church
(8). Return parallel (9), noting characteristic Georgian pedimented doorways (10) and a Venetian doorway opposite, to Gothick
porch on clustered shafts (11); nice houses (Venetian window)
round corner (12). Back past Town Hall (13) to fine balustraded
house (14), across town to c19 palazzo bank (15). s to c18
Assembly Rooms (16), stone house (and mill buildings). n past
shell doorways and Gibbs surrounds (17), good corner group (18),
w to irregular Old Town area and n to pilastered Custom House
facing dock.

Also in the Lake District are two delightful urban villages. At
Cartmel, good townscape: from priory church past c18 house with
9 round windows (keystones) to cross and square (little loggia,
bow windows); then Georgian houses with good doorways—half
right towards racecourse, and through medieval gateway (high
ogive windows). *Hawkshead* has an intricate plan; alleys (with
houses over), slates on walls. Explore from old school with twirly

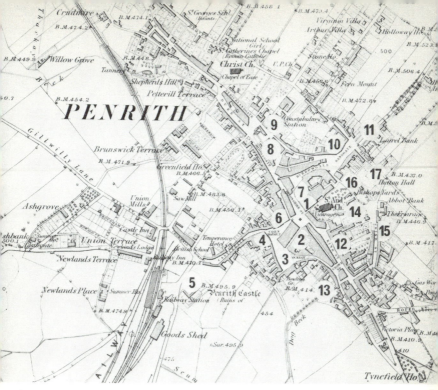

door s of church, to little squares: by old town hall (round windows in recesses) with timberframe house in corner; and to bank with pargetted door, Gothick hood moulds, Venetian window.

Penrith (1867): a largely Georgian market town (segmental doorways) with an intricate plan and spaces. Start at market place (1). First up lane (2) past strange 1763 house with double Venetian plus ogive windows to c18 houses/pubs (3), to (4) and castle (5). Back past 3 rusticated pilasters (6) to (1). Then past good shopfront, white stone house opposite 'George' (7) to fork: left, c17 school (8) opposite columned bay window, and fine sandstone house (9)—gatepiers, Venetian window; right, to pleasant street (10) and 1815 chapel facing house with Venetian windows in wings (11).

Then s from (1) past 1776 columned bay windows and rusticated pilasters (12), and house with varied windows (ogive, round, Venetian), to more columned bay windows (13). Finally from (1) by pilastered bank to good houses (stone oriel window) round church, fine Georgian (14) with pediment, c17/18 houses (15), and two fine houses: (16) with Venetian windows in wings and Gothick link and wall niches; 7-bay sandstone (17) plus c15 pele tower.

Kendal (1863): basically a good main street (good shopfronts, bow windows) with nice alleys and courts off. From bridge (1), church—6 windows wide; mansion/museum (2) with recessed Venetian windows; good group (3)—shell door, loggia, gabled timberframe; then left, stone pair, house plus brewery now theatre (4), 1659 arch to almshouses, pilastered 1833 bank (5); to Town Hall (6)—1820s rusticated windows, columns. Then (7): on left, timberframe, pilasters, loggia; right, hotel pedimented windows—followed by timberframe (spiral door columns), rebuilt Moot Hall with Venetian window (8), next to delightful little Market Place. Becomes tattier, but good Georgian 7-bay (9) opposite house dated 1724.

Two good loops. First to best two courts and 'fellside' up from (5), under houses (10), to nice green (11), motte and bailey castle (12); past (10) up cobbled lane (13), back along Old Shambles (14) with pedimented and pilastered end. Secondly from Market Place (8), to delightful New Shambles (15), down cobbled lane (16) past C18 gates and C17 cottages, to 13-bay terrace (17) with tripartite windows over rusticated arches, pilastered corner (18) with recessed porch, 1794 bridge (19) and medieval hallhouse (20). Return past terraces (21) behind church, pilastered villas (22)—laurels, bow window. Back across river, by (23) to 1818 bridge and approach house (24), quayside house (25) with tall round windows, to end with Georgian Lowther Street (26)—bow windows at ends, curious surrounds, factory plus figure, Gibbs doorways. Good expedition E to canal area (27) and castle ruins (28).

Brampton: a nice mixture of stone and brick, with good loop from cobbled area round octagonal market hall (Gothick windows, clocktower); past pub tripartite windows to church, returning along main road (Gibbs doorway, pediment, Ionic porch), across intricate area to Georgian redbrick house with segmental windows.

Alston: from Georgian houses (good doorways) and hotel below C19 Gothic town hall, up past C17 group (1681, curious dormers) on left (plus cottages up lane) to steep cobbled area and good houses round market cross.

Appleby: good Georgian from bridge and then into superb wide Boroughgate—from arched and castellated church screen and column (Low Cross) up to grass, trees, similar High Cross and castle. On left, sandstone house, late C17 gables with finials, C19 banks, riot of ogive windows (plus door), bargeboards, C17 almshouses with cobbled courtyard. On right, island Moot Hall (large first floor windows, bell turret); first and second floors on cast-iron columns; segmental doorways on club, corner of house and 7-bay beyond; nicely varied Georgian (door roses, ogive porch). Nice minor Georgian houses off Boroughgate to W and in parallel Doomsgate.

Kirkby Stephen: a long irregular main street (and spaces) worth exploring S from Perpendicular church tower. Georgian (good shopfronts) with some late C17. On left cobbled Market Square, 1810 pediment and columns screening churchyard (good house to E), 1663 rusticated pilasters, pub bow windows and porch, lively 1903 bank; out to 1856 Temperance Hall with bloated figure. Right 1636 lintel, groundfloor castellations, more rusticated pilasters, bay window with columns.

Carlisle (1868): first explore in detail surprisingly complete Georgian area SE of castle (1)—between Inner Ring Road (2), cathedral (3) and Market Place (4), with four good streets: (5) with walls above river and cathedral precinct buildings; (6) with 1689 Tullie House (museum) with broken pediments above its windows, good doorways, odd first floor tripartite windows; (7) with stone terrace and purplebrick houses with broken pediment doorways; (8) is part pedestrian, houses with tall Doric and Ionic pilasters, and eaves curving out over bowfronts, Georgian chequerbrick. Attractive Market Place (4) with C14 timber Guildhall, C17 cross and C18 Town Hall with clocktower — behind it an inn with quoins and Venetian window (9), opposite the Lanes area being redeveloped.

To late C19 commercial area (10) with fine banks leading to station, like Inverness; past C19 Assize Court round towers and neo-Georgian crescent (11) into 1830s area. Excellent stone buildings — pilastered bank next to strange long church windows, opposite little terrace and double bow window (12). Then brick row with stone doorways (13), and terraces — of stone with Ionic porches (14) and brick (15). To s, nice 1880s Portland Square (16, since map) and an extensive mid C19 stone and purplebrick residential area (17) with columned doorways and round fanlights. (Similar terraces over Eden bridge towards Scotland). Huge 1836 stone cotton mills (18).

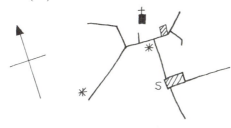

Kirkby Lonsdale: delightful, largely stone. Start at Market Place — battlemented cross, good hotel, pilastered C19 bank, row with bow windows and columned shopfronts. E to good house. s with more good shopfronts, pediment/gable with tall sidewindows opposite bay window over Tuscan columns, gatepiers (and to splendid medieval bridge). Then N: little terrace opposite pedimented bank, right to C17 house and column/cross in cobbled square, 1700s with segmental doorway, nice row. Back to fine 1854 corner (*) — pilastered, rusticated, with recesses; and to lunette windows (Gothick glazing) in gables over tripartite windows (repeated thrice) opposite little loggia and C18 iron church gates (amazing Norman arcade in church). On bend, 5-bay with pedimented doorway — as up street, at top of which C17 Abbot Hall (*). Round to right to good pub, doorways and 1825 neo-C17 houses with many gables and finials.

County Durham

Durham (1861): a few streets to explore—characteristic Georgian purple/red brick with some stucco, to supplement great Norman cathedral, castle (university) and precinct. w of medieval bridge: good new infill shopping centre (1), good houses near church (2) and facing cathedral (3). Street rises nicely up to Market Place (4)—Georgian stone surrounds, classical c19 bank.

Beyond new Inner Ring Road and bridges (5) Georgian houses along and off street to E (6).

Explore city on rock in great detail: good street up (7) has on left two classical facades with Doric door columns, right timberframe—up to sumptuous early C18 doorway (8) facing green. Round loop (9), continuously fine Georgian with good doorways, including C17 shell doorways and some stone (one grand rusticated house). Back and across bridge with medieval prison in abutment (10) to fine Georgian street (11): pilastered hotel, brick and stucco (pedimented) terraces, nice iron balcony, to triangular green (12). Past 1800s courthouse (13) with portico (and gaol), to more brick Georgian (14), looking at new Arup footbridge (15). At fork: left, medieval priory barns (16) opposite 1700s house with stone bands; right more Georgian (17). Pleasant riverside walk, with views, round (18) to (3).

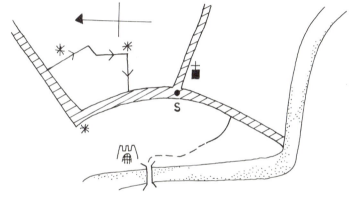

Barnard Castle: a moorland town with many good stone C17 and Georgian houses. Sally in 3 directions from octagonal C18 market/town hall (niches, Venetian windows). First E past church (trees, house with 6 tripartite windows) to RC church and glimpse of incongruous C19 French style Bowes Museum. Then down to river: on left C16 house with 3-storey bay window, Georgian dated 1742, C17 house (huge first floor windows, tiny second, crude Ionic doorway); only one C18 house now left in Bridgegate, but ahead trees, C18 mansions, mills. Finally N up winding wide street—left 'Golden Lion' dated 1679, right excellent 3-storey Georgian and pedimented hall. By C19 Gothic church (*) with castle behind, up wide Galgate with trees: left, two white roughcast houses; right, Georgian bay windows, rambling roughcast house with 5 round windows (3 tall, 2 small). Nice loop into King Street (stylish lettering on corner) past two good houses (*), back by alley into main street.

Lancashire

Clitheroe has a nice street from little keep on hill to town hall, with an excellent group (pediment) near church.

Lancaster (1848): black stone Georgian houses often with big window and door surrounds. Best area round and below castle (1). To sw (2) 16-bay terrace, stables (round windows) to grand houses with segmental doorway, entrance pediment high above columns, doorhood. Then pedimented dispensary (with balls), down past cottage with 1730 lintel (3), warehouse with hoist, tripartite windowframes, to cobbled area next to fine C17 Judge's Lodging (4); up to church (5) past good houses (scroll doorway). Below (4) to bow window and grand house with good doorway (6), beneath new offices/carpark well scaled down (7) to C17 pub (8) and

splendid c18 warehouses (9), terraces, custom house with portico. Back to fine frontage (10)—keystones, two pedimented double doorways (side Venetian window), past gaps, to screen (pedimented wings, double pilasters) facing (11) c18 bridge.

Back past c18 church tower/spire (12) to pedimented house (13) and another double doorway. Then corner Venetian doorway and windows (14), 9 tripartite windows, and square (15)—with a good pair (16) and magnificent neo-Baroque Town Hall (17)—since map. Pedestrianised (18) to delightful square (19) near Old Town Hall with portico and cupola, unexpected Renaissance Music Room (20) in lane, Georgian street (21)—nice shopfront, keystones, to pilastered c19 banks (22). Finally s via (19) to Assembly Rooms quoined window and circular porch, delightful c17 almshouses (23), good frontage (24) with pub segmental door and aprons, to cobbles and good houses (Gothick glazing under pediment) of square (25) and street (26) with twirly top to pilastered double doorway. Up (27) to grandest terrace (pedimented) and fine 5-bay house (28).

Northumberland

Away from *Newcastle* (not covered being a historic city), a marvellous, sparcely-populated county, with some of my favourite historic towns.

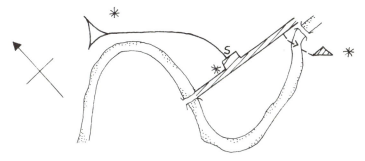

Morpeth: a mixture of stone and purplebrick, with Scottish influence seen in island town steeple (*) and good new infill housing (*). Start at widening (Market Place), opposite Vanbrugh's Town Hall (rebuilt). N up good curve, then gaps, good houses—on left, first floor and groundfloor recesses—to fork. W past Town Steeple to Georgian Collingwood House, bridge, nice sharp edge. Finally E down commercial street with pub bow window and remodelled chantry—beside which, path over piers of old bridge to good houses, castle-like 1820s Court House (*), and castle remains in park.

Berwick-on-Tweed (1862): alternately in England and Scotland (as can be seen in the style of the houses), with its complete Elizabethan walls 'one of the most exciting towns in England . . . with the strongest sense of enclosure . . . red roofs on grey houses and the most intricate changes of level' (Pevsner). From station (1) on site of castle, good houses in street (2) to Scotch Gate (3). First walk round the walls: down to 1920s and C17 bridges (4), past custom house and good view of Sandgate (5) to 1820s terrace (6) facing estuary, back round bastions (7), with views on to barracks (8) and church (9). For the keen, on to NE corner for original wall of Edward I (10). Then into walled town. From (3) to commercial street (11) and Town Hall (12). Back down good street (13) to (4), past fine Georgian houses (14) to sloping street (15) with good hotel (Venetian windows). Then

Sandgate (16), to step back into an C18 barrack town: to green (17) and strange Governor's house (with both gables and pilasters—influence of Vanbrugh?) up once fashionable street (18) to Vanbrugh's bizarre barracks (8) and unusual C17 church in green (9). Then good houses (19), one with 2 Venetian windows, back to (12) and to E (20).

Alnwick (1867): apart from famous castle and park, it has splendid townscape—hilly, dense and urban, many good C17–19 houses, almost all of stone, with careful new infill and good sharp edges to town. From column (1) through gate (2) into good street becoming wide with cobbles towards arched and columned island hall and nice Market Place, through under 1771 Town Hall to street with pilastered house (3). Good houses uphill (4) beyond gaps. Down lane through arch near fountain (5) to attractive early C19 classical stone residential quarter (6) near church. Back to (5), explore rest of central triangle. Out to delightful C18 Gothick Pottergate (7); back past impressive houses and castle walls (8) to main entrance. Then spacious street (9) to church; and down to bridge (10).

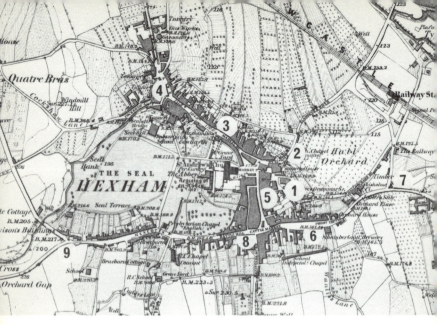

Hexham (1865): an irregular street pattern and many fine C17 and C18 houses—most stone but some brick. Explore from Market Place at E end of splendid priory church (new nave since map) with good houses and open market building. First through C15 Moot Hall to equally sinister C14 prison, and C17 school (1), and Georgian brick houses. Secondly through funnel opening downhill (2) and back to good street (3)—symmetrical C17 house with bay windows and open pediments, priory gate, grand Georgian house, hood doorway; past gaps to stone house dated 1657 (4). Thirdly pedestrianised (5) to Priest Popple (6): house with Gibbs surrounds on every door and window, and early C19 classical out to (7). Back to street with good Georgian houses of brick and stone (8), out to fork (9).

Yorkshire

York is not covered, being a historic city—nor *Kingston-upon-Hull*, with a good historic area near its huge Holy Trinity church. The present North Yorkshire, taken from previous North Riding and rural N of West Riding, is a marvellous county—with attractive countryside, fine historic houses, abbeys and churches, and delightful towns. These include towns not covered later: Regency and early Victorian *Harrogate*, and the much smaller *Malton* and *Kirkbymoorside*; *Yarm* (now in Cleveland) with strange pilastered houses in its main street; *Hedon*, see page 19, now in Humberside; *Settle* with excellent market place and irregular spaces and islands—up to fantastic C17 Gothick Folly; *Bedale* with nice main street up to the Hall facing church; the delightful spaces and houses of *Middleham*, and cobbled market place and island town hall at *Leyburn*. *Thirsk* has market place with islands, cobbles, and two good inns (3-storey bay/Venetian window), and good Georgian houses N to grand Hall and Perpendicular church.

Skipton (1854): largely blackish stone. Start at bottom of splendid wide High Street (1). First E to little terrace opposite pedimented Georgian inn (2), early C19 houses with recesses and Ionic porch (3), past gaps to nice C17–18 group (4) with old school. In High Street Georgian rows (Gothick doorshaft) on left (5) of island (C18 Tolbooth pilasters one side, blocked arches the other), and on right (6) with pilastered bank. Beyond, tripartite windows combined into huge Venetian, stucco, 1862 Town Hall portico, to fine house with Gothick shafts on porch and bay windows (7), castle entrance (8). On left nice group (one 1676) and curve (9), two pubs with good doorways before and after bridge, stone cottages to sharp edge of town (10). Good loop along canal arm towing path—looking across to cobbled streets (11), past junction (12) to converted warehouse with crane (13).

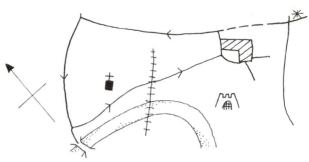

Knaresborough: dramatic site above river, attractively varied townscape in Market Place area at top, and many fine black stone buildings, including some grand Georgian houses. Best tour is long loop shown: from bridge, up steep cobbled lane to church, under railway to Market Place area and castle gardens. Beyond bus station to stateliest house (*), then back down High Street to bridge.

Ripon (1856): a pleasant town with nice plan, of Georgian brick with timberframe. Minster only made cathedral in 1836, so no close, but to s grand house (1) and excellent c17/18 group with

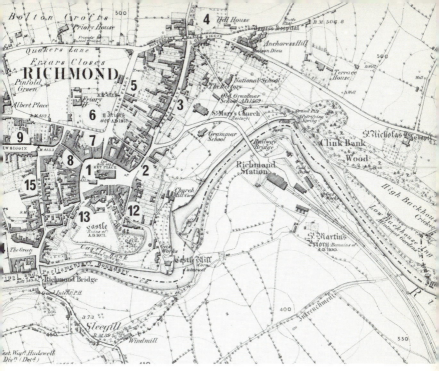

chapel, 7 round windows, Gibbs surround; to N classical courthouse, C17 houses (3) and (4). Street (5) winds nicely — with some good houses (6) to S, to large Market Place (7) — with obelisk, pedimented 1800s Town Hall, carved timberframe next to 'Unicorn'. Sally out: S through rundown minor Georgian to little stone terrace (8); to W C18 (9) to good group (10), and pleasant early C19 street (11); up both streets (12) N, with good Victorian area beyond — to clocktower (13) and leper chapel (14).

Richmond (1857): with its Norman castle keep, a superb hilltown to explore in great detail. Some amazingly grand C18 houses — purplebrick or stone, some stucco. Start round cobbled Market Place (1) — island chapel, Town Hall, obelisk. Past good houses at bottom (2) down into Georgian street (3) — fine porches, columned bay windows, up to house (4) with Venetian windows, back via pedimented house with lunette window (5), Greyfriars tower (6), and lane through arch next to Georgian theatre (7). Out again through (8) to wide Georgian Newbiggin (9): Gibbs surrounds opposite delightful Gothick bay windows (10); and little square (11). Back to (1), good lane (12) with raised pavements next to castle. Finally good loop down to bridge: marvellous materials and textures through gate (13), to village-like green (14), back up cobbled street (15).

Whitby (1853): a delightful historic port, with many C18 houses and characteristic purplebrick and redtile roofs. First and most picturesque, E of bridge: narrow lane (1) with double bowfronts, rusticated ground floor, pilastered 4-storey house; S with nice brick and stone amid new housing to C19 almshouses (2) and good group uphill (3); back past overhanging timberframe, along brick and stucco street (4), to sculptural steps (5) up to extraordinary pew-filled church and ruined abbey (6); beyond, little terraces (7) with bands, segmental windows, and view of strange Doric column/lighthouse. Return under Town Hall, opposite (4), with Venetian window and cupola, past 7-bay stone front, to bridge.

W of bridge, first N: custom house, and nice rounded corners (8), warehouse and pedimented redbrick Georgian house with Gibbs windows, to stucco pilasters and bow windows (9) facing Fish Market. Back to street (10) commercial, but with houses of Georgian brick, fine stone (aprons, surrounds), C17 stone, early C19 inn, Gothick church, segmental windows at back of 'George'. Then C17 mullioned house (11), opposite fine Georgian houses above gardens—stone, brick, pilasters, pedimented centres, to elaborate window/door and terrace (12) with Gibbs windows, 3-storey ironwork. Up to grand terrace (13) with, at back, stone

porch, Venetian window, row with parapet raised at centre (14). By C18 mansion above corner conservatory down pleasant mixed street (15) to steps; or to 1850s West Cliff and stucco terrace (16).

Pickering (1854): good moorland town—stonebuilt, redtiles but some Georgian redbrick. From E: some grand houses—bow windows (1) opposite rusticated pilasters; fine inn (2); good (3) to new bridge. Main town to N: to green with redbrick pair (4); up street to redbrick house (5) with garland doorway; through delightful churchyard, past two shallow bow windows to nice space (6) and good street (lunette windows) to castle (7). Nice steps (8) down to station. Back to (6) and Georgian redbrick house with recessed Venetian windows, rusticated pilasters, lunettes. Down Market Place (9)—bow windows, quoins, to medieval bridge and Georgian house (10) plus tall Gothick windows; good grassy street (11) back to main road (12).

Helmsley: small-scale, nearly all two-storey, grey/yellow stone houses with redtile roofs. Spacious Market Place has best houses (medieval timberframe) near church; attractive walk S to grander C18 house and bridge, then N along stream, past entrance to castle, to edge of town.

Stokesley: by contrast with Helmsley, it is basically purple/red brick, three-storey at centre, many houses having a pair of bow or bay windows. Marvellous townscape sequence from E to W. Square with islands (C19 school) and stone manor house next to church; Market Place in front and both sides of 1854 Town Hall—with fine C18 inns. (Across packhorse bridge to attractive riverside area). Then good houses round green—the best Georgian with side pavilions, white keystones and quoins—to C18 cottages and grand house with fluted pilasters at edge of town.

Scarborough (1853): a popular seaside resort with splendid gardens and sands, but also an extensive historic town with characteristic purplebrick bow windows and thin columned doors. Along harbour (1): amid fish and chips and bingo, old custom house, Georgian brick and bow windows, medieval stone mullions, redbrick pair, to Georgian redtiles (2); behind it C17 pub (roundels), timberframe (3). Up to C18/council area—past chequerbrick house (4), round church (5) to redbrick terrace (6) with round windows and pilastered ends. Along greens to bow windows (7), and behind to bow and bay windows and stucco terraces (8). Back past 1836 almshouses (9) and down to door with urns (10); good Georgian (11) E to pedimented double doorway (12) and W (13), down past cross (14).

Main spine and to s. Georgian houses above road (15); road straightened since map; huge coffered porch (16); Market Hall (17) with recesses and rusticated pilasters—facing street (18) with good group (segmental surrounds plus Gibbs door, stone balustraded, fanlike window tops). Off N good street (19) with triglyph bow tops out to familiar purplebrick (20). In streets opposite: good house (21); fine Georgian (pilasters, segmental windows) and old Town Hall (22) with recessed centre; High Victorian (23) to lavish Grand Hotel (24); bow windows and fine stone library (25) with columns and wreaths; 'typical' terrace (26) to climax—1830s stone 24-bay terrace (27), 45-bay crescent (28), finished in 1857 (after map), recessed, pilastered, continuous iron balconies, with pilastered bow windows between (29). Beyond fine station and Methodist church, 'typical' houses for some distance. Back to Crescent and three fine golden stone villas (30), above 1829 rotunda (31), to early Victorian stucco terrace. Across valley to similar South Cliff development: bow windows (32), pilasters, recesses, central portico, ironwork, columned porches (33).

Beverley (1855): formerly East Riding, now Humberside. Besides marvellous Minster, many Georgian houses of characteristic purple or redbrick, with tall thin doorways often

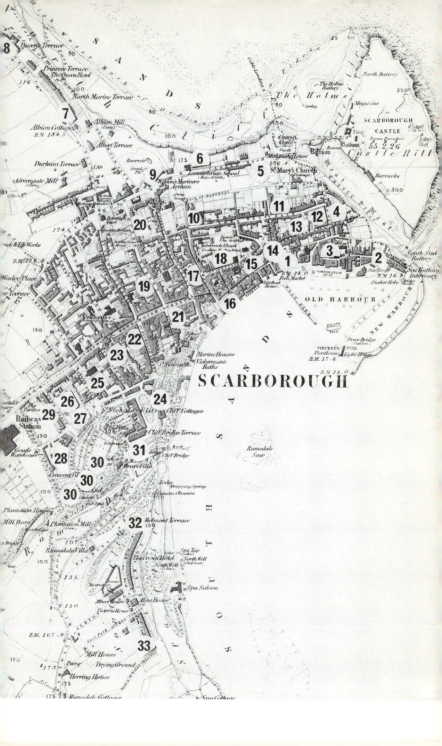

8

Queen's Terrace

Princess Terrace
The Queen Hotel

North Marine Terrace

7

Albion Cottage
B.M. 184.5

Albion Mill
(Corn)

Albert Terrace

Durham Terrace

Greengate Mill
(Corn)

Wesley Place

Terrace

B.M. 128.8

rick & Tile Works

20

9

Wilson's Mariner's
Asylum

6

Lancasterian School
Boys & Girls

5

St Mary's Church
Vicarage

Molson House

10

18

11

13

12

4

14

15

1

3

2

South Steel
Battery

Sea Bathing
Infirmary

B.M. 16.9

Docker Hole

19

17

16

OLD HARBOUR

NEW HARBOUR

21

ISLAND
PIER

Draw Bridge
Cast Iron

22

VINCENTS
PIER

Light House

VINCENTS
Pier House
B.M. 17.6

23

Marine House
Vickerman's
Baths

B.M. 15.0

25

SCARBOROUGH

26

24

Nick Slack & Co
Cliff Cottages

Ramsdale
Scar

29
Railway
Station

27

Cliff Bridge Terrace

28

31

Cliff Bridge

30

30

Grove Villa

Lodge

Spring

30

Camera Obscura

Plantation House

Mill Dam

Plantation Mill
(Corn)

32

Belmont Terrace

Ramsdale Villa

The Crown Hotel
South Well

Spa Tap
North Well

B.M. 167.9

Spa Saloon

Albert
Victoria House

33

Mill House

Drying Ground

Herring House

SCARBOROUGH CASTLE

The Holms

North Battery

SCARBOROUGH
CASTLE

55.2.26

Castle Hill

Barracks

pedimented—like Boston. From attractive Saturday Market Place—good island corner (doorhood) and shopfronts facing 1714 Market Cross; good spaces s (1) with 8-bay pair and double bow shopfront, and N (2). Beyond gaps to 5-bay house with urn (3) opposite blank arches; and segmental doorway (4). N to elaborate pedimented house (5)—gatepiers, rustications, round window-tops with garlands, through nice area (6) to splendid St Mary's and fine inn porch (7). Then trees and cobbles, C15 exposed timberframe, 14-bay terrace with 'typical' doors (urns) and delightful narrowing to 1409 North Bar (8). Outside: broad with trees, Georgian interspersed with mixed Victorian, out to 1800s portico beyond (9).

Back past (7) to good Georgian area (10); past delicate doorways and 7-bay 1690s to bar house (11); pilasters and pediment, blank arches, *greybrick* (12) and grand C18 Hall (13). Across green into nice Georgian area w and N of Minster: almshouses (14); villa with Gothick doorway (15); street with Gibbs doorway (head) and stucco lodges (16), recessed arches in pedimented almshouses and terrace. Round Minster to Friary (17), past good frontage (18) to irregular Wednesday Market Place (19). To E, nice 1840s terrace (20). N commercial (21) but stucco door columns, keystones, serpent shopfront (22)—whence to stucco villas with columns in recesses (23) and row to guildhall portico (24).

11 Scotland

Introduction

Being based on the English Midlands and never having lived or worked in Scotland, I visit Scotland as an outsider and am very aware that I may make mistakes or miss points that a Scot might recognise. Nonetheless I wanted to cover both Scotland and Wales, as many people (including the natives) seem to think of them primarily for their mountains and scenery rather than for their towns. Scottish historic towns (apart from Edinburgh) have tended to be underrated.

Because Northern Scotland was originally a tribal society and the land was not rich agriculturally, where there are any towns at all they are often planned towns, laid out to a grid by a local landowner—and now usually with a public lavatory on the axis! Only around the coast are there towns with medieval plans such as are common in England. Whereas in the Centre and South, historic towns like this *are* found, with a hinterland of country to feed them—Perth, Linlithgow, Dumfries and smaller towns like Kirkcudbright and Jedburgh.

So what are the 'Scottish' characteristics of the towns, and their buildings? The most striking feature to me (born in East Anglia) is the almost universal use of the 'queen of materials', stone—which makes the individual buildings handsome, but the towns perhaps a bit dour and lacking in the textural variety to be found in most English towns. I even like the common Dumfriesshire red sandstone, which earned the scorn of a Dundee friend, who likes to go to East Anglia to see cottages built of cob and thatch. Then one notices in the suburbs single-storeyed bungalows, rather than the usual English two-storeyed house, and conversely in the centres a high proportion of people in stone blocks of flats, making the medieval parts of Edinburgh and Stirling high density areas reminiscent of some French towns.

Architecturally there is the medieval Scots baronial type— compact, castle-like, with round corner gables, and later the 'traditional' c17 houses seen at their best at Culross—the 'little houses', roughcast over stone walls (usually painted white now), stone windows, often with outside steps to first-floor living areas, and with 'crowstep' side and/or end gables. In the c18 the windows are still stone (often painted black, contrasting with the white walls), but the steps are gone, the ground floor is used and there are fine Georgian doorways or Venetian windows. Often there are still gables to the street elevation, and in many 'fisher towns' there are rows of cottages — usually one-storey only — presenting their endgables to the sea. Among public buildings of the C17 and C18, the Tolbooths and Town Houses in Scotland (unlike their equivalent in England) nearly always have towers and/or spires like Gibbs' St Martin's in the Fields in London.

The C19 is chiefly striking for the quality of its school, town hall, and bank buildings — usually classical, but later Baronial or Gothic revival — built to a higher standard than in England. Many of the larger towns have fine Victorian residential areas, with stone villas and avenues, well-cared for today. These buildings are often later than the First Edition 6″ maps used (ranging from 1854 to 1874). In the C20 while there have been the usual tower blocks, and bad commercial development by chain stores, there has also developed a modern Scottish vernacular style for public housing — irregularly grouped, three or four storeyed white roughcast, with pitched roofs and triangular end gables, which I find pleasing. It blends in well with the older buildings.

So, while Scottish towns may have fewer different materials and textures than the English, or have fewer historic and Georgian buildings, they have more varied silhouettes and skylines — often seen against a backdrop of woods and hills.

I have not covered Edinburgh, Glasgow, Greenock and Aberdeen, (but see page 13) and I have grouped the towns in areas, journeys, rather than in administrative units.

Central Scotland

Musselburgh: main street with Georgian houses leading nicely to the widening round the cross and conglomerate Tolbooth. Good riverside houses including one (w bank) with a remarkable dome of 1776, Gothick windows and urns. Visit nearby C18 urban village of *Inveresk*.

Dunbar: High Street with curious polygonal Tolbooth tower and fine Georgian houses — from SE by church to NW next to magnificent Lauderdale House; good C18 houses by old harbour.

Stirling (1865): castle on hill, medieval houses, stone tenements and classical residential areas. Main historic streets from chief shopping street (1) up to castle (8). First stretch with good banks and C18 'Golden Lion', split by curving C18 Burgh Buildings with spire. Right: tenements with a good house set back (2), leading to splendid wide street (3) with 1701 Tolbooth, cross, C17 houses.

Left: 1530 house with scissors inscription (4), to good Georgian street (5) crowned by French-style apse of magnificent Holy Rude church and C17 hospital (6). Routes uphill join at ruined C16 Mar's Work (7), past magnificent C17 Argyll's Lodging to castle (8).

Good loops for the energetic. First from (3) past C17 ruins (9) and good new housing, good Georgian in streets to right (10) including grand pedimented, and (11), out to fork (12); returning down main street—blitzed at first, later minor terraces (13), pilasters (14), up pleasant curving street (15). Second, from public buildings (16—since map), Town Hall (17) to two excellent slightly different classical terraces (18) and villas (fine double doorway); round to column/clocktower (19) and fine C18 house with pediment and urns. Above tree-lined road (20) detached C18 houses and neo-classical semis, and similar but later avenue (21)— part of good mid C19 residential area (22).

Haddington (1855): a superb historic town, mostly Georgian stone, and well looked after. Wide Court Street has good public buildings on s (1) and excellently detailed Georgian houses — including one with pavilions, urns and sphinx (2). Then the Town House, an attractively restored traditional close (3) and to fine houses — pedimented with Ionic pilasters (4), and early C18 white gabled (5). S to another restored close (6) and good houses to dovecot and C16 bridge (7), and splendid recently restored church (8). Back past a fine C17 house (9), a stretch of town wall (10) through another restored close (11) into superb High Street. Regular, wide, with cross and many original shopfronts, vistas closed by neo-baronial facade of hotel. Classical stone island bank beside palatial front of Carlyle House (12).

Linlithgow (1856): the attractive High Street and The Cross (1) have many good C17–18 houses and several old fountains. The Cross has old Town Hall and County Hall, by lane to superb church and palace (1). High Street good: E to (3); W past nice curve and extensive white West Port redevelopment (4). Higher up to S: good C19 classical stone houses facing railway (5), and higher again, along canal (6).

Dunblane: some nice roughcast historic C16–18 houses round the cathedral and in The Cross.

To the English Border

Lanark (1864): an attractively irregular centre. In High Street Doric doorway of old bank (1), C18 Court House with rounded windows. SE: classical shopfronts (2). Beyond church on island (its tower is owned by burgh) to street with finest houses. S side: stucco 'Clydesdale' (3)—with columned porch, tri- and quadri-partite windows; house with one pilaster; 4-column doorway. N side: another pillared doorway, nice curved corner (4) with shopfront. To N fine public buildings culminating in splendid Palladian County Hall of 1836 (5) opposite an early C19 house with tall Egyptian splayed doorway and windows. Outside town: C12 ruins of old church (6); to SW by the Clyde, Robert Owen's remarkable 1800s industrial hamlet of New Lanark.

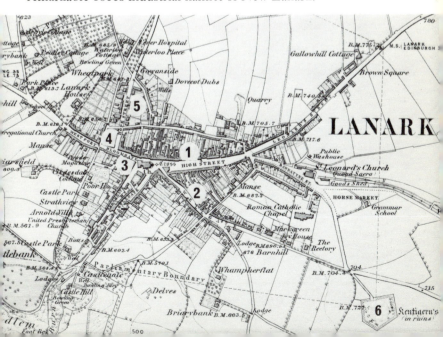

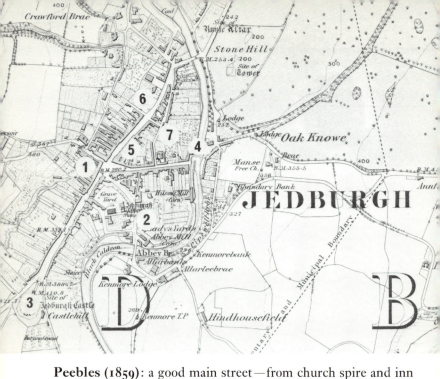

Peebles (1859): a good main street—from church spire and inn
(1) to open spire of church at end (2). S side: C17 house (museum),
C18 old Town House with pediment and urn, Georgian painted
inns, 1759 gabled building with ogive window. N side: pilastered
shopfront and good stone house. Over Tweed Bridge to good view
of town. Good loop over stream (3) to Old Town, two historic
birthplaces, former pub with lion on doorway (4), and out to
ruined friary (5). Over stream into Northgate (6) with good C18
houses and 1693 'Cross Key Inn', and to remains of Town Walls
(7). Their line continued past (1), (8), (2) and along stream.

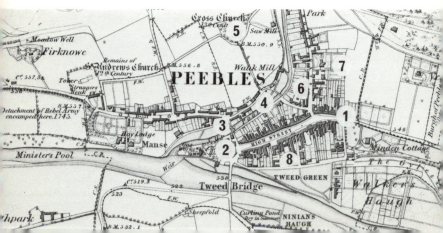

Jedburgh (1863): many medieval traditional houses. Next to irregular Market Place is a restored group with closes behind (1) while c18 gateway with spire leads to superb ruined abbey (2). Uphill to gaol (3) on site of castle. Down to medieval bridge (4) past good early c19 hotel and another medieval group. Good High Street (5)—basically 3-storey with good classical houses, banks and inns (one with double classical doorway) to grand mansion setback (6); lane down to c16 Mary Queen of Scots' house (7) isolated in garden.

Kelso (1863): an exceptionally unspoilt Georgian town, with sharp edge formed by river. From fine 1803 bridge (its twin pillars characteristic of Rennie) marvellous townscape sequence: white stone screen of the fine c12 ruined abbey (1), bend, street (2) opening into Market Place with fine Court House. Many pilastered shopfronts—fluted Ionic in (2), Doric elsewhere; superb white c17 house (3). From Market Place by (4) to good houses beside Post Office. By (5): pilasters on left, past good houses and octagonal church to c19 house with portrait bust (6). Along (7) to detached Georgian houses and little terrace facing river (8); to classical mansion (9) near church, past pilastered terrace and good houses to Floors Castle drive (10).

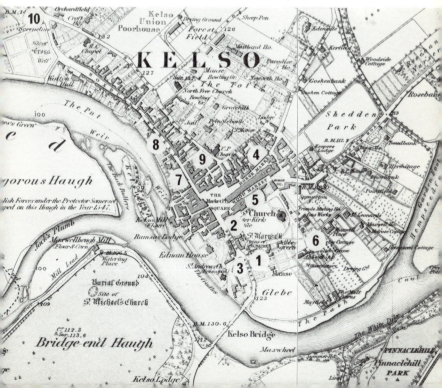

Selkirk: attractively situated on a hill, presenting from the bridge a good skyline of towers, spires and baronial county buildings. Market Place has good inns and old Court House with spire and statue of Scott. Up High Street another triangular space with good houses round Mungo Park statue.

Biggar: a main street with good houses (initialled marriage lintels over doorways). From packhorse bridge at sw: C17 gable with delightful scrolls (also on endgables), good doorways (classical, Gothick). After green towards church, street widens, with trees. On left: irregular frontage with islands—Georgian black and white inns, an elaborate parapetted porch, rusticated ground floor, classical shopfront, finally groundfloor remnant of grand C18 house—opposite good classical doorways and house beside turning.

South-west Scotland

Ayr (1860): a thriving shopping centre, largely redeveloped, but still much to see. From New Bridge next to double bowfront (1), fine street up to splendid 1828 Town Steeple (2) with twin angle columns, scrolls and spire/obelisk—Baroque compared with sober Georgian frontages below; beyond, good shopfronts and handsome banks. Two good loops to right. First: past doorway (3), to isolated house with another double bowfront (4), C16 Loudoun Hall (5). Second, up street (6) to classical churchfront. Left, terrace with good doorways; right, traditional gable with chimney/columns, pedimented house with Venetian doorway; past classical (7) to St John's tower and terrace (8)—part of fine 1870s development of Cromwellian Fort.

Back to site of gate (9). s past shoddy area to excellent Georgian quarter (and beyond it Victorian villas); a square (10) and portico and rotunda of County Buildings (11); good street into square (12); terrace with rusticated groundfloor (13). Back to (9), past four Venetian windows on corner (14), E to emerge at island in High Street—in lively, largely Victorian townscape. Right to 1832 Wallace Tower (15) and Burns' 'Tam o'Shanter Inn' (16); left, to cross cobbled Auld Brig (17) to river quay (18) and 1795 church steeple (19) of once separate Newton-on-Ayr.

Wigtown: has a spacious central triangular green, from its two burgh crosses—near good C18 houses (pediment)—to Victorian County Buildings, and attractive street down to church and sea.

Whithorn: pleasant long main street winding uphill—with good houses near tower and arch to priory.

Dumfries (1861): a thriving centre, with central planning blight. From New Bridge (1) into mixed street (2) culminating in Victorian Greyfriars on corner—centre of town. Nearby: Georgian street (3)—ironwork over steps; fine classical bank with figure in niche (4); Venetian windows and Egyptian shopfront with fluted columns (5). To space (6) with C18 island Trades Hall and 1707 Mid Steeple, and good Georgian fronts and inns near iron fountain (7). Left, along nice winding street (8) with good doorways and shopfronts, pediment/gable, composers' busts, out to Queensberry monument and Victorian County Buildings (9). Return, noticing Georgian street (10).

From (7) past 'Globe' through blighted area to grand pedimented house (11), Burns House (12) and Mausoleum (13). Back from (11): a Baroque facade (keystone, Gibbs surround) behind wall (14); early C19 stucco and little terrace with good fanlights (15); triglyph doorway on corner of good street (16) opposite stucco columns; pediments (17), becoming 3-storey Georgian. Follow (18) to river. Explore lively but tatty quay area and cross C15 bridge (19) to windmill and Grecian museum (20)—in the old county of Kirkcudbright and so ignored by the OS cartographer!

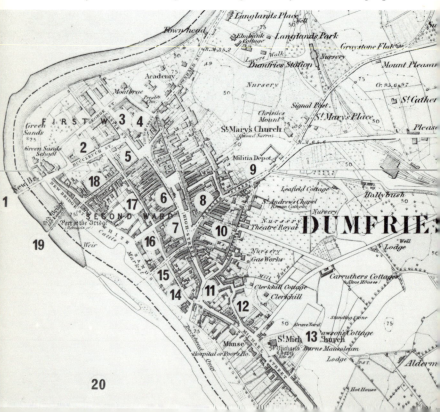

Kirkcudbright (1854): a delightful little town. From pictures-que harbour and ruins of C16 castle/mansion (1), L-shaped High Street with many good C17–18 houses: three pairs of slender fluted pillars on doorways; fine Blair House (2) with wide doorway and castellated back (see from side lane; good view from wooden pier); house with oval window above doorway with elaborate surround; good doorways—rusticated semi-Gibbs, Venetian and pediments both sides; C16/17 Tolbooth, cross and stone range with nice close behind (3); C19 Court House; good fanlight and pilastered ground floor of 'Gordon Arms'; shallow two-storey bow windows (4) plus castellated annexe (good fanlight) and 'Selkirk Arms' (where Burns stayed). Then marriage lintel (5) and detached C18 house (6). Back down nice two-storey Georgian street (7)—good doorways and shopfronts, as also in (8), and (9)—shopfront with Corinthian columns. N of bridge (10, since map) good new vernacular housing.

Fife

Cupar: a market and former county town. Mostly yellow sandstone, three good streets meet at the Mercat Cross at centre. w: minor Georgian terraces, 1811 Masonic Hall, c17 gables, out to fine stone c17/18 houses with wide classical doorways facing each other. E to park—past bowfronted Town Hall on corner, Georgian houses with hotel facing the Adam-like terrace of 1815 County Buildings. To s: first commercialised but wide with setts, later excellent Georgian residential, to nice sharp edge of town.

Dunfermline (1856): a thriving, large burgh—industrial but with medieval street plan, some good buildings. From splendid Norman abbeychurch (1): first to ruined palace, Gothic gateway (2) and Andrew Carnegie's birthplace (3). Back by (2), following winding Maygate (4) with good c16 and c18 houses to good Georgian (Venetian doorway) ahead and right (5). An attractive c19 residential quarter (6) beyond. Up across High Street (7) with 1808 County buildings plus steeple and good classical banks (and terrible Co-op tower) to more Georgian houses and pubs (8). Then from (9) down High Street to splendid 1890s Flemish municipal tower (10), and curving park entrance (11), up street (12) with pleasant houses, to 1930s Glen Bridge (13) with view of town.

The almost continuous little historic coastal towns and ports of Fife (really only villages now) are famous for the traditional 'little houses', many restored by the National Trust for Scotland — white roughcast, stepped gables, with outside stairway to first floors, often marriage or other inscriptions on door or window lintels.

Earlsferry has good High Street inland and no harbour, whereas *Elie* has 'little houses' along shore, attractive area by harbour, and spacious street with green and Georgian houses inland. In *St Monance* little houses are clustered nicely round harbour, but more strung out in *Pittenweem* — which has lively harbour, is more urban and has an attractive town street inland — with trees and little market place near church.

Anstruther: bigger, with larger harbour. At w end, little houses and church form an attractive open square with the sea; behind, in High Street, two houses adorned with shells, Town House. Good East Street (behind fisheries museum). Then good James (up to Tolbooth), John and George Streets, next to (but not along) the sea, lead to little houses round harbour (and one block inland) of *Cellardyke*.

Crail: with a good group of little houses (cobbles, redtile roofs) by tiny harbour, but a surprising number in the spacious streets (with trees) inland — plus grand Georgian, island Town House, early c19 mansion near collegiate church.

Culross: the most famous of all, but on the Forth w of the two great bridges. Largely restored by NTS; with its cobbles, intricate textures, white walls, stepped gables, dormers and towers, it has the unreal perfection of a film set — a Scottish Williamsburg. Explore area by estuary in leisure and in great detail; then uphill to fine collegiate church.

Falkland: my favourite of the Fife group, but inland — the little houses having particularly elaborate inscriptions. Explore from Renaissance palace past Tollhouse to good group beyond baronial Savings Bank; return along higher street to corner house dated 1663.

St Andrews (1855): two main historic streets — North and South — lead to the cathedral (1) (ruined, little left) with Market Street in between; a general impression of stone textures — in walls, arches and gateways.

Start at medieval area (2), up to impressive castle ruins (3), past splendid buttresses of medieval university church (4) to

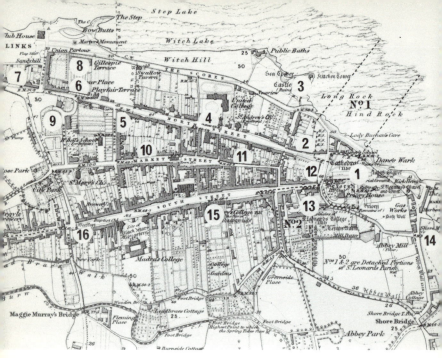

Edinburgh-like terraces (5) and (6); good C19 classical houses further out (7) and to seafront (8). Then into excellent mid C19 residential development round garden (9), into Market Street—commercial at first (10) near cross but later (11) narrower and more domestic. From medieval houses (12) lane leads through Gothic gateway to St Leonard's (13), along priory wall through another arch (14) to harbour. Finally from (1) the best, South Street—with contrasting C16/17 gables, C18 houses with good doorways, and colleges—go into courtyard of St Mary's (15)—getting more commercial towards 1589 West Port (16).

From Perth to Aberdeen

Perth (1866): a fine historic town with a central medieval core girdled by early C19 'improvements' facing outwards to the green North and South Inch either side.

Historic core. From new bridge and 1820s county buildings with twelve Doric columns (1), into street with many fine historic houses up to (2), back to 'Salutation Hotel' (3) with huge Venetian window, flanked by soldiers. Into excellent street (4) with C19 bank palazzi, more Venetian windows (one house has six), and around the great church. Into High Street whose E end (5) is also relatively undeveloped: s side, c18 row with little Gothick windows at top; N side, wide rusticated doorway dated 1699. Explore to (6) and to river, past pilastered corner (7) to street with further c18 houses. Then along splendid approach street (8): on left, elaborate window surrounds, green dome of classical museum; to Smeaton's 1771 bridge (9).

Early C19 'improvements'. From (9) along North Inch: grand c18 houses (10), s to Fair Maid's House (11), more formal terraces (12) and (13)—pilasters between houses, and a pedimented crescent (14). Then grand terraces (15)—rusticated groundfloor, fine 1807 Academy as centre; round to street (16) half formal, half villas. Across town via library (17) and impressive mill building, streets (18) and (19), to splendid c18 hospital (20) with wooden cupola; past good classical semis (21), to emerge at South Inch. Along this: terrace (22); 1885 church, open spire; spectacular 1801 Marshall Place (23) (grand corner, 5 houses, centre, 5 houses, corner, all twice); to splendid 1830s waterworks rotunda (24) with column/chimney surmounted by urn.

Dunkeld: urban village, famous for its square and street up to the cathedral, restored by NTS—C17/18 white and yellow roughcast, stone window surrounds. But it is equally attractive (and more varied) beyond road crossing (splays on four corners); and left to splendid Georgian hotel on columns, or right to similar hotel, good houses facing river and Telford's fine stone bridge.

Montrose: nice houses along harbour. Excellent main street from bridge up past Georgian houses round curve to wide High Street, confident church tower and spire and 1763 Town House, jutting out with statues either side. Explore both sides in detail (good shopfronts) and alleys off to where street narrows. To E: street to classical church portico; and path from Town House past church to classical civic area—museum, mid C19 Glasgow-like Panmure Terrace with first floor ironwork, and 1815 Academy with dome capped by gold roof.

Arbroath: N part of High Street, near ruined abbey, though pedestrianised, has little left; but s part has good commercial and civic buildings (explore area round old Town House). To E Hill Street and Terrace have classical houses and library; C18 houses near harbour.

Brechin (1865): from cathedral (1) with round tower, attractively hilly and irregular streets worth exploring: street with C18 houses (2); out to (3), back up to (4) and (5), down to nice widening (6) by 1789 Market Hall, down to fork (7), near modernised medieval castle (8).

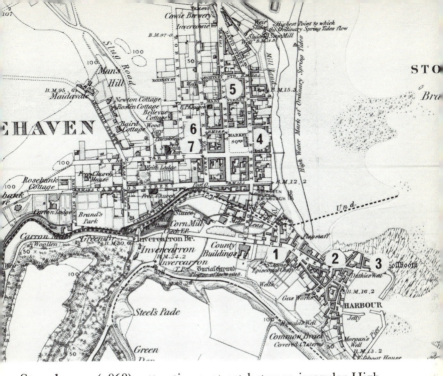

Stonehaven (1868): attractive contrast between irregular High Street (1) of Old Town—with Mercat Cross and c18 steeple (2) and c16 Tolbooth (3) on quay, and c18 gridtown to N. Explore: Town House with rounded tower/spire facing Market Square (4); fine regular street (5); to c18 house (6) with doorway on fluted columns; and two good c19 stone classical banks (7).

From Aberdeen to Inverness

In the extreme NE are two lively fishing ports, both planned to a grid. *Peterhead* has good Broad Street, with an excellent c18 house at harbour end (3-storey bow windows at back), Doric column and 1788 Town House with spire—and good classical granite in the streets to s lined up with them (and in St Andrew Street between). At *Fraserburgh*, from Saltoun Square (old cross, stumpy church spire, rounded corner of council buildings) runs another Broad Street with good classical corner bank; from here to harbour past high round window.

By contrast the urban village of *Portsoy* has an irregular plan, c18 roughcast houses next to tiny harbour—as in Fife; explore inland—up Low Street and North High Street to The Square, with late c18/early c19 houses of a more familiar type.

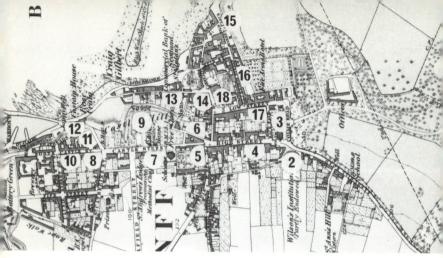

Banff (1871): an excellent historic town with varied buildings—in orange sandstone, white roughcast, granite and even with Georgian inns painted black and white as in Wales. Smeaton's 1779 bridge, amazing Baroque mansion (1); classical Academy (2); Doric Lodge (3). High Street (4): c17/18 houses, some with gables; parish church steeple, fine setback houses with fanlights; left to c18 curved gable (5), attractive to right (6). Then fine mid c19 classical buildings (7) culminating in Doric portico (8) opposite c18 mansion (9) on site of castle. Late c18 houses ahead (10) and right (11). To good warehouses (12), custom house, and roughcast cottages along shore. To fine house (13) with wide porch on slender fluted pillars; Gibbs surround beside c17 corner turret (14); textures and shapes of old churchyard opposite. Then to largely Georgian Old Market Place (15), along (16) to Low Street: to 1843 'Fife Arms' facing 1870 County buildings (17), then back past grand houses, fine classical bank (near nice lane uphill), cross, and climax of c18 Town House and Steeple (18).

Then a rash of Georgian planned grid towns—*Tomintoul, Dufftown, Huntly*, plus *Cullen* refounded in 1822; and the three that follow.

Grantown-on-Spey: explore spacious square with trees and old Town House, and main road 100 yards either side—with attractive grey granite Georgian and Victorian houses.

Fochabers: moved from original site by owners of Gordon Castle. An urban village with a nice, regular main street: SE to NW, from church with spire to inn with Doric porch—past the Square, with classical church (portico, spire) between arcaded houses; balanced by Gothic facade of episcopal chapel opposite.

Forres: walk excellent High Street from NE end at 1823 Institution with spire and gateway between Doric columns: good classical stone buildings, inn with first floor ironwork, little cobbled area by strange Danish-style Tolbooth tower, 3-storey classical palazzo, gabled houses (one pair either side of classical bank), ambitious St Lawrence's, view of obelisk at SW.

Nairn: good High Street from good corner buildings at Gordon Street, past 1818 Council Offices, redstone Highland Hotel to 1815 monument—with excellent C19 stone classical in between. Also sally out to its delightful harbour and Fishertown; and the unique townscape/landscape of *Fort George*.

Keith (1871): as the map shows, *two* regularly planned settlements. Mid Street (1) with Georgian inns (one black and white painted dated 1762 on lintel) and Town House (cupola) leads to square (2); past good houses to church with bulbous green dome (3). Over river, Fife Keith has good houses, particularly where shown as (4).

Elgin (1873): a major historic town. Splendid ruined cathedral (1), precinct gateway (2), C16 bishop's house (3), C18 house, now library (4), good new housing scheme and arch (5), fine dome (6) like Four Courts, Dublin; medieval Greyfriars chapel (7). Excellent High Street—from 1733 Little Cross (8): good historic houses on arcades (blocked) with elaborately carved dormers; new arcade linking through to (5); Mercat Cross, island church with classical round tower (like St Pancras new church, London) above severe portico, C17 house with corner turret (9). Fine C19 stone commercial buildings (and reasonable infill): round church; W out to steps to Tuscan column on site of castle (10); up street (11) framing church tower; beyond, good C19 residential quarter (12). Finally beyond (13), magnificent 1815 hospital (like University of Edinburgh).

The Highlands and Islands

Generally not of course an area of historic towns, and where they exist the problem of remoteness arises. On extreme W and SW is the urban village of *Inveraray*—perfect townscape, laid out beside Loch Fyne in 1740s by the Duke of Argyll, with regular white houses leading to Palladian church (spire removed in 1940s), and, at right angles, to handsome Court House. To the South,

Rothesay, on the Isle of Bute, and *Campbeltown* are apparently worth visiting—but I haven't.

Inverness (1874): the Capital of the Highlands, with much to explore, despite decay and gaps along river and too bulky redevelopment in centre. First famous riverside walks from bridge (1): to contrasting blocks of new theatre and Victorian cathedral (2); across suspension bridge to good Regency and Victorian houses (3), church, and, uphill behind it, tiny 1815 dome (4); fairy-tale castle (5); new development and car park with C18 houses in front (6), three fine spires, historic houses (7), over second suspension bridge (8); N to some grand Georgian houses (9), back past four churches (10)—classical, neo-Gothic, neo-Baroque and modern.

Town centre. From (1) to High Street (11) with classical terrace and good Victorian classical and Baronial buildings including Town House. Then first (12) of C19 streets centred on 'Station Hotel' (13)—looking left down second (14) and splendid Queensgate (15, since map) and looking right at church (16) to Doric portico (17). Down lane to emerge by 1668 Dunbar's hospital (18) with elaborate dormers (as at Elgin). To historic houses round churchyard gateway (19), back past C16 house (20), (14) with market arcade, to Tolbooth Steeple (21).

On the Black Isle, *Fortrose* has good houses round its ruined cathedral aisle, ranging from Town House bow windows to vernacular elsewhere.

Cromarty: a delightful historic port, now an urban village, with a wealth of C17/18 buildings ranging from Court House with cupola (near Hugh Miller's house) and grand house with gatepiers, to small irregular cottages with gables facing the sea.

To N and W, *Dornoch* has a pleasant cathedral green with bishop's palace (in no sense urban) and *Ullapool* was attractively laid out to a grid in 1788. I never managed to get as far as *Tain* and *Thurso*, *Stromness* and *Kirkwall* in Orkney, and *Lerwick* in Shetland, but all are apparently worth exploring.

Acknowledgements

The Ordnance Survey maps are reproduced by permission of the Syndics of Cambridge University Library. The line maps were drawn by Philippa Hall. The extract on page 20 from Dr W. G. Hoskins' *The Makings of the English Landscape* (1955) is reproduced by kind permission of Hodder & Stoughton Limited and the quotation on page 24 (from a BBC talk in 1957) by kind permission of Dr Hoskins.

I should like to thank many local authority planning officers for their help and comments, especially those in Scotland and the archivists of the Counties Corporate; and in particular: Paul White for his constant encouragement and his amazing skill in putting on, and lifting off, numbers on the maps; Mr K. L. Winch and Mr G. D. Bye of Cambridge University Library for assembling the map material; the University of Birmingham Arts and Research and Study Leave funds for grants towards the travelling costs; James Bond of Oxfordshire County Museum for help on town defences; David Lloyd and the Ludlow Historical Research Group for information on Ludlow; the Royal Commission on Ancient & Historical Monuments in Wales for help on Welsh town defences. In common with almost all recent topographical books, this one owes a debt to Sir Nickolaus Pevsner's *Buildings of England* series, which exhaustively records the buildings mentioned briefly in this book. And finally I should like to thank my wife Zette, for drawing the architectural details, keeping my study sacrosanct, and for considerable ingenuity in amusing three young children in a large number of historic towns, with historic playgrounds.

Index of places

Towns not included in the CBA list (see pages 6 and 11) are listed in italics.

Towns included in the CBA short list (see page 7) are listed in capitals.

Places in the CBA list but not discussed in this book are listed without any page number.

The CBA references on pages 17 and 29 are not to its 1965 list but to its follow-up 1972 booklet *The Erosion of History*.